The Styles of English Architecture

Hubert Pragnell

The Styles of
English Architecture

Hubert Pragnell

B.T. Batsford Ltd. London

For Charlotte and Christian

Half-title page Charlton House, south London, 1607-12.

Frontispiece   King's College Chapel, Cambridge, 1446-1515.

©Hubert Pragnell 1984
First published in 1984

ISBN 0 7134 3768 5

Printed in Great Britain
by Butler & Tanner Ltd
Frome, Somerset
for the Publisher
B.T. Batsford Ltd,
4 Fitzhardinge Street,
London W1H 0AH

Contents

Acknowledgements

I would like to acknowledge the help and encouragement of a number of colleagues at The King's School, Canterbury, including Mr Paul Durgan who provided a number of photographs of material in Canterbury, Mr Raymond Butt who could always provide a quick answer to obscure points of railway history, and Mrs Lucy Ross who very kindly found time to type the manuscript of this book on top of the demands of being a mother, and housemaster's wife.

I also thank Dr Morris Crosland of the University of Kent who has been very enthusiastic about my inclusion of architectural examples from northern England, and Dr and Mrs Peter Livesey who have helped with certain textual points, and finally my wife Dorothea who has been most helpful and encouraging during the writing of this book.

Hubert Pragnell

The Author and the Publishers are grateful to the following for their permission to reproduce the illustrations: J. Boulton, photograph 26; Paul Durgan, photographs 2, 11, 18, 21, 23, 24, 25; A.F. Kersting, FRPS, photographs 1, 4, 5, 8, 9, 12, 16; Lever Brothers, 22; Eric de Maré, photograph 17; Royal Commission on Historical Monuments, 10, 13, 15; Reece Winstone, photograph 20.

Foreword

It has often been said that architecture is the most lasting record of history and the needs of our ancestors. We are surrounded by it, whether our environment is Georgian Bath or twentieth-century Letchworth. To understand the reason why our home town or village appears as it does, one must have some knowledge of the various architectural styles and their influences. Few places exhibit only one building phase, except new purpose-built towns, and even these are gradually changing to accommodate the needs of society. In older towns old buildings give way to new, or an office complex is developed in a suburb which hitherto has been largely rural in character. However, in recent years, conservation groups have become increasingly successful in rescuing whole districts from decay or demolition, and so preserving the historical atmosphere for the benefit of future generations.

Inevitably a book of this size can be no more than an introduction, and I am aware that the work of some architects hardly receives more than passing mention; for instance Robert Adam deserves far greater treatment, so also his contemporary Sir William Chambers, and Sir John Soane is omitted altogether. Equally, twentieth-century movements are so numerous that they cannot receive justice in the space available.

As so much has been written about various aspects and periods of English building, it is hard to strike a note of originality in such a general work, so I ask the reader's forgiveness for the reappearance of the familiar yet again. On the other hand, since architectural style is forever changing, and buildings are created for a specific purpose as an age requires, they may well change their appearance over the centuries. A new nave may be added to a church, a wing to a mansion, or another storey to a college quadrangle, and so, where appropriate, I have tried to show the original appearance of a façade, and how it appears today. Hampton Court gateway is an example of one of the most well known of English buildings to have undergone radical alteration, during the eighteenth century. I have used contemporary drawings or engravings for making my own illustrations of these examples.

With a knowledge of architectural styles it is possible to 'anatomise' a building, and so to build up a continuity of development to within several decades, which is vital if there is no documentary evidence on which to fall back. Also it is possible to see how styles inspire, or repeat themselves over the centuries. For example, the late eighteenth century saw the Gothic revival, as well as the renewed interest in Greek culture which led to an archaeological approach to stylistic interpretation, based on the study of original examples of ancient architecture. St Pancras church in Euston Road, London, is directly inspired by the Erechtheum in Athens. This century has seen the revival of the Queen Anne and Georgian styles, and even French Gothic used as the basis for Giles Gilbert Scott's Anglican cathedral at Liverpool.

Where appropriate I have tried to link the development of English architectural styles to those of our Continental neighbours. The British often tend to think of themselves as an island race, yet they are as much part of the European tradition of architecture as France or Germany. In any case the achievements of, for instance, Inigo Jones are meaningless without reference to Renaissance Italy. Indeed, Rome became almost an obligatory place in which to study for any aspiring architect in the eighteenth century, starting with James Gibbs at the studio of Carlo Fontana, a leading late Baroque Master.

Whilst I have tried to include the widest possible representation of examples of building and detail from across the country as well as several from Edinburgh and North Wales, it is inevitable that I have been selective. Many of the examples therefore have been chosen from close personal acquaintance, but unavoidably some major buildings have been left out due to lack of space.

It is hoped that this book will tempt the reader to get out and look at our environment, though obviously some towns and villages are richer in outstanding buildings than others. Outside London, the university cities of Oxford and Cambridge are probably the best places to see the full range of architectural styles from the late Saxon period to the present day. Though covering a much smaller time-span, Liverpool has over 1000 listed buildings and one of the finest nineteenth-century city centres remaining in Europe, in spite of extensive damage during the last war. At the end of the book I have included a list of towns in each English county which are worthy of careful study, though it is a personal selection.

Often a walk off the main tourist route or local high street will bring its surprises and rewards. Even the grounds of a country mansion may be rich in architectural content reflecting the taste and leisure of an aristocratic family; or in the solitude of the Yorkshire dales you may find the remains of an early Gothic Cistercian abbey.

If this book succeeds in making the reader more aware of our environmental heritage it will have achieved its purpose.

I

Anglo-Saxon architecture c. 600-1066

The period of English history between the withdrawal of the Roman legions and the invasion of the Normans has received more scholarly attention in recent years than ever before. However, in spite of this the label 'Dark Ages' must remain, especially for architecture, since successive waves of invaders tended to destroy all but the most substantial buildings.

Little is known of fifth- and sixth-century Anglo-Saxon life. Until recently it had been thought that the population settled away from major Roman sites, as is the case in St Albans, where a settlement was made on a hill to the north of Verulamium. On the other hand archaeological evidence proves a continuous occupation of London, Canterbury, and several other regional centres. Often these Roman sites were exploited as useful quarries for most materials necessary for ordinary buildings, although away from towns, wood was invariably used.

In *Beowulf* we learn of great communal halls in which local chieftains held court, but only post-holes have come to light through excavation to confirm their existence. It is to churches that we must turn for evidence of the Anglo-Saxon style, and even here hardly any survive without substantial alteration. Some scholars divide the period into two: from the re-conversion to Christianity up to the Danish invasions of the ninth century, and from Dunstan's religious revival of the mid-tenth century – coinciding with the Ottonian renaissance in Germany – up to the Norman invasion.

1 Saxon detail
Brixworth, Northants. c. 680.
Detail of south wall showing Roman tiling used in arch of doorway. Herringbone masonry pattern used above on either side of window.

Below right
Greenstead-Juxta-Ongar, Essex. Tenth-century original nave of split timbers incorporated within later reconstruction. The chancel is built of brick.

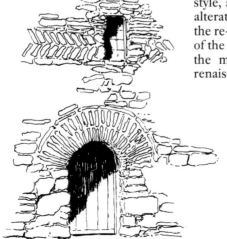

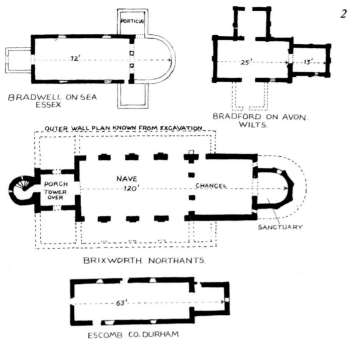

Whilst St Martin's, Canterbury, may claim to be the oldest surviving centre of Christianity in England, evidence of its original appearance is lost, apart from the western wall of the nave. Excavations at the nearby Benedictine Abbey of St Augustine have revealed a church plan consisting of a series of rectangular compartments ranged round a large central chamber. This type of layout can be seen better at nearby Reculver which had an eastern apse divided by two columns which are now preserved in Canterbury Cathedral. It is thought that these Kentish churches were built by Frankish masons and may derive from examples in northern France.

The side chambers were known as 'porticus' and may have originated in Italy as burial chambers, or places for private devotion. The finest example of a church from this period is that of Brixworth, Northants., of about 670, although here the eight porticus on either side of the nave have been destroyed. Since columns were obviously hard to carve, the dividing arches rested on piers. The sanctuary to the east of the nave is terminated by a polygonal apse, a form which may derive from Ravenna. Both the interior and exterior show extensive re-use of Roman brick, and in the western tower there are courses of Saxon herringbone ornament. Another early church is at Bradwell-on-Sea, Essex, *c.* 600, of re-used Roman masonry from the adjacent fort.

3   Bradford-on-Avon, Wilts.
Chapel of St Lawrence, between
800 and 1000, complete apart
from southern porch.

After the Synod of Whitby, 663, Roman Christianity was confirmed in the north leading to considerable church-building in stone, including Benedict Biscops' monastic churches at Jarrow and Monkwearmouth where, according to Bede, masons from Gaul were employed. Jarrow originally had four porticus down each side of the nave. Otherwise northern churches tended to be tall and narrow with two-cell plans as seen at Escomb, also in Co. Durham. Several northern churches had crypts such as those built by Bishop Wilfrid of York at Hexham and Ripon, which still survive.

The Danish invasions destroyed much from the preceding centuries, and it was only after Dunstan's monastic revival and strengthening of the English Church from about 950 that any further significant buildings survive and then none in their original form. The little Saxon church of St Lawrence at Bradford-on-Avon is probably a tenth-century remodelling of an eighth-century building. Cruciform in plan, although now missing the southern transept, it is worthy of note for its crude blind arcading along the nave and chancel walls. As with all Saxon structures the windows are small. At Bradford, as well as Deerhurst, Glos., there is evidence to suggest a weak attempt to create fluting at one side of an arch, and as window decoration.

Several towers survive from about 1000; most notable is that of Earls Barton, Northants. Of rubble masonry, it is decorated with vertical strips of stone and a band of crude lattice-work, bearing a loose affinity with Lorsch in the Rhineland. The belfry openings are noteworthy for their bulbous columns. The corners are dressed with the characteristic long-and-short masonry found elsewhere. Affinity with the Rhineland is also shown by the 'Rhenish helm' tower at Sompting, Sussex although without any Continental elaboration, such as bands of corbel arcading.

The church at Greenstead, Essex, is the only Saxon building remaining in wood, and then only the nave walls of split tree-trunks, probably the normal method of house-building as well. This church is said to have been built in 1013 as a resting place for the remains of St Edmund on their way from London to Bury St Edmunds, although there is no positive evidence of a date of construction. By this time the greater churches were coming under increasing Continental Romanesque influence. Canterbury Cathedral had a western choir – common in the large Rhineland cathedrals, and neighbouring St Augustine's Abbey received a rotunda, inspired by that of Saint-Benigne, at Dijon.

It is unlikely that any Saxon work was comparable in magnificence to Continental buildings except perhaps Edward the Confessor's Westminster Abbey, which was then largely Norman in style and inspiration. Traces of ornamental carving are plentiful but primitive in design and shallow in depth of cutting. However, what the Anglo-Saxon period may have lacked in architectural magnificence was more than made up for in the visual arts, especially illumination and metal work, such as was revealed by the treasures of Sutton Hoo.

4B Deerhurst, Glos. Saxon
window, eleventh century?

5   Saxon towers.
Sompting, Sussex. Early eleventh-
century Rhenish helm tower with
German example from Limburg am
Lahn.

Earls Barton, Northants. c. 1000
showing loose ornamental affinity
with monastic gate at Lorsch near
Worms, c. 830.

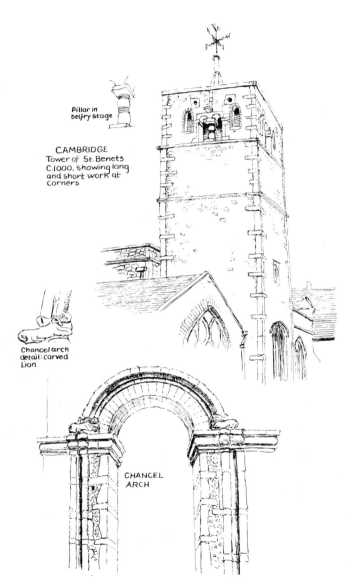

Pillar in
belfry stage

CAMBRIDGE
Tower of St. Benets
C.1000. showing long
and short work at
Corners

Chancel arch
detail: carved
Lion

CHANCEL
ARCH

6   *Saxon, St Benet's, Cambridge.*

II

The Normans 1066-1175

Although the Normans finally invaded England in September 1066 under Duke William, their influence in architecture had been felt for many years before. Indeed Westminster Abbey, which was the major preoccupation of Edward the Confessor, was a building heavily influenced by Norman Romanesque planning and ornament, with a nave twelve bays in length. It was gradually demolished from the 1240s to make way for the present building. Although the invasion was successful, resistance against the Normans was fierce, especially in the north; therefore the early years of William's reign were not a time of extensive building.

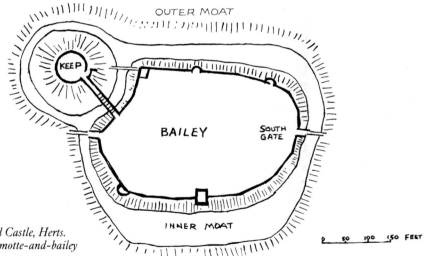

7   Berkhamsted Castle, Herts. c. 1080, simple motte-and-bailey plan.

The first requirement was stability in State and Church, and so, soon after the invasion, castles and fortified enclosures of wood were erected at strategic points. The simplest form was a 'motte-and-bailey' plan, where a wooden wall surrounded a man-made earthen mound crowned by a wooden stockade. Obviously these could only be regarded as temporary, and from the late eleventh

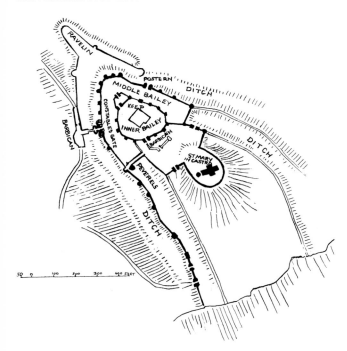

8   *Dover Castle, Kent. Remodelled between 1168-88, late rectangular keep with fully developed curtain wall system.*

century they were replaced by enduring stone keeps. The first was probably the White Tower in London, followed by the keeps of Colchester and Rochester. By the later twelfth century all castles had been converted to stone.

We must remember that a castle was the house of a nobleman and his family who held the estate as a pledge of loyalty to his sovereign. It would also accommodate a garrison and even act as a prison. Keeps were sometimes up to ninety feet in height and over one hundred feet square. Walls were up to fifteen feet in thickness and faced in many cases with great blocks of dressed stone. The first few feet of the building were splayed for stability as well as defence. Entry was by means of a wooden staircase to the first floor which could be dismantled in time of danger. A keep such as that of the White Tower, or Castle Hedingham, had up to four storeys; the lowest storey was a basement used for stores and pierced by narrow circular openings. It would also contain a well, essential for water if the garrison were under blockade. The hall as in the White Tower occupies two floors with a chapel on the east side terminating in an eastern apse. Domestic apartments were ranged on each floor, the lower for the constable and officers of the garrison, the upper for the king and his household.

The White Tower was heavily restored in the early eighteenth century, but we can still gain an excellent impression of its strength. The exterior is of Kentish

9   *The White Tower, c. 1080.*
Although heavily restored in the
eighteenth century it remains the
finest example of a Norman keep in
England. It is also the earliest in
stone and was supervised by
Gundulf, Bishop of Rochester. He
used Kentish ragstone for most of
the exterior wall surface although
harder limestone from Caen was
shipped across the channel to provide
ashlar surrounds to the windows
and dressing for the buttresses.

UPPER FLOOR

COUNCIL
CHAMBER

HALL   CHAPEL   UPPER FLOOR

              CRYPT   ENTRANCE FLOOR

STOREROOM   SUB CRYPT   BASEMENT

ragstone with the walls divided by tall, slightly projecting buttresses dressed at the corners with ashlar Caen limestone. The windows are semi-circular-headed, now nearly all enlarged to the size of the inner recess. The summit of the walls is battlemented and the corners crowned by turrets with lead caps. The least altered part of the White Tower is the chapel of St John with its beautiful ashlar drum piers, cushion capitals, mortared barrel vault and eastern apse. It was probably only after about 1100 that the first defensive system of stone walls was erected, broken at intervals by mural towers to allow for visual cover of the ground immediately beyond the enclosure.

10   Variations on the Norman keep plan.

Windsor Castle. The Round Tower, an excellent example of a Norman shell keep. The right half shows its original appearance prior to alteration in 1826.

Orford Castle, Suffolk, built in 1166.

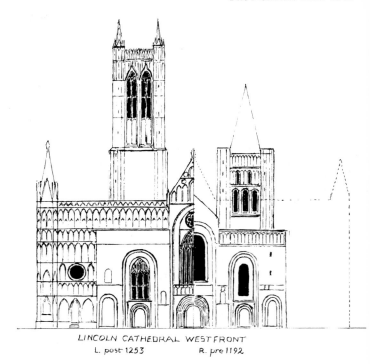

LINCOLN CATHEDRAL WEST FRONT
L. post 1253   R. pre 1192

11   Lincoln Cathedral.

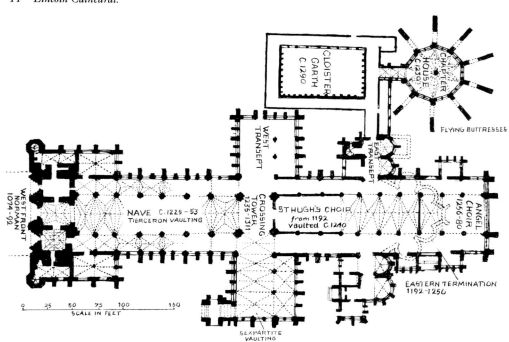

CLOISTER GARTH C.1290

CHAPTER HOUSE C.1230

FLYING BUTTRESSES

WEST TRANSEPT

EAST TRANSEPT

NAVE C.1225-53
TIERCERON VAULTING

CROSSING TOWER 1235-1311

ST HUGH'S CHOIR from 1192 Vaulted C.1240

ANGEL CHOIR 1256-80

WEST FRONT NORMAN 1074-92

EASTERN TERMINATION 1192-1250

0   25   50   75   100   150
SCALE IN FEET

SEXPARTITE VAULTING

Besides the rectangular keep plan the Normans also built octagonal tower keeps such as Orford and Conisborough. Another variation was the circular shell keep as at Restormel, Cornwall, and at Windsor. Many Norman keeps suffered alteration in the later Middle Ages, or were slighted during the Civil War and thereafter became a quarry for local building material; Canterbury and Colchester – the latter itself using building material from the Roman township of Camulodunum – are examples of Norman keeps considerably reduced in height due to the removal of stone and rubble for building elsewhere.

Besides establishing a strong military government the Normans reformed the English Church, gradually replacing prominent Anglo-Saxon clergy by foreign bishops and priests. Perhaps the best example was the removal of Stigand the Archbishop of Canterbury who had crowned Harold king in January 1066, so denying William his claim to the throne. He was replaced by Lanfranc who, Italian by birth, was Bishop of Bec in Normandy. No sooner was Lanfranc installed at Canterbury than the Saxon cathedral was damaged by fire. He quickly inaugurated the rebuilding, executed between 1070 and 1077, on a plan similar in size to the Abbey of La Trinité, Caen. Canterbury might be said to have begun the Norman programme of cathedral rebuilding. It was followed over the remaining decades of the eleventh century by Norwich, Peterborough, St Albans, Winchester, Worcester, Gloucester, Lincoln and Durham.

With the exception of Lincoln these cathedrals formed part of monastic complexes and so had a range of conventual buildings arranged round a cloister on the south or north side of the church, in a layout devised at least as early as 820 for the Abbey of St Gall, Switzerland. A typical Norman abbey or cathedral would be cruciform in plan with a long nave, up to fourteen bays in length as at Norwich. The monks' choir beyond the crossing might be another five bays terminating in an apse with the side aisles forming a processional ambulatory. The nave and choir elevation would be nearly equally divided between the lower arcade, triforium and clerestory. The arches of the lower arcade might be supported on thick piers with attached shafts, or alternatively on thick cylindrical drums with a variety of incised ornament as seen at Durham, Selby and Waltham. Until the late twelfth century vaulting was rarely used in England over naves and choirs, being confined to side aisles and crypts. Durham Cathedral was the exception where the earliest rib vault in Europe was constructed over the choir in about 1100, just a few years after the massive groin vault of Speyer in Germany. Durham also exhibited pointed arches in the transverse ribs of the vault, but England was to remain generally faithful to the semi-circular arch until the late twelfth century.

The cruciform plan normally introduced one set of transepts, but under the influence of the Abbey of Cluny in Burgundy, eastern transepts were introduced at Canterbury and Lincoln. Like the French, the Norman builders in England preferred two main western towers and a lantern tower over the crossing between the nave and choir. St Albans and Winchester Cathedrals retain the somewhat squat early ones, whilst Norwich has a rather mature example richly decorated and surmounted by a later spire. The two western towers at Lincoln are decorated with bands of ornamental arcading, some of it blind. They were enlarged in the fifteenth century.

Many of the ornamental features found in the great Norman cathedrals can also be found in the numerous parish churches which survive from this period of great rebuilding. Churches tend to be of two basic plans: either cruciform with a central tower, or two-cell, that is a simple nave and chancel ending in either an apse or a square end, the latter more prevalent in the north. Clerestories are rare, the side windows being the main source of light. If the

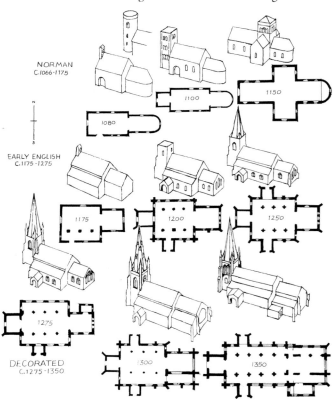

12   The development of church planning from the Normans to the Reformation. These are not specific examples but incorporate typical features from each period. See also Chapter V.

church was in a main township it might have side aisles, though these do not tend to appear much before the middle of the twelfth century. Doorways were usually on the south side. Kilpeck, Herefordshire; Stillingfleet, Yorkshire and Barfreston, Kent, have excellent examples of these, whilst Iffley near Oxford has a richly carved west doorway, with an abundance of chevron moulding. Buttresses as in military architecture were thin strips acting as no more than wall divisions. Sometimes the walls were topped beneath the eaves by a corbel arcade which might also cover the roof gables as well.

The Normans loved extensive carved decoration not only round the joints of doorways and windows but also on chancel arches. The most common forms of moulding are chevron and beak head, but cable is often found round large arches such as the crossing arch in Southwell Minster. Another form is known as billet moulding. Frequently capitals were carved with a mixture of plant forms and grotesque monsters eating each other's tails or playing musical instruments, as in Canterbury Cathedral's western crypt. The semi-circular-headed block over a doorway known as a tympanum might contain stylized plant

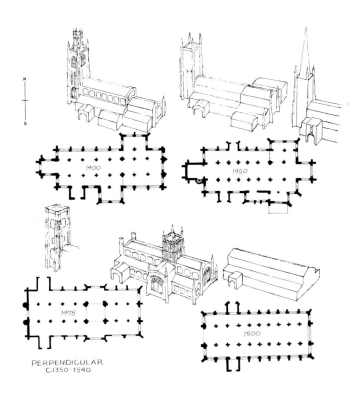

PERPENDICULAR
C.1350-1540

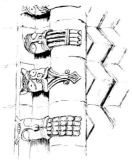

13A   Norman ornament. Beak-head moulding from Iffley, Oxon. (above) and Lincoln Cathedral (below).

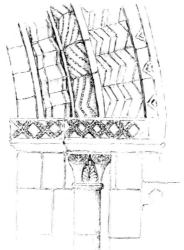

13B   Norman ornament. Patrixbourne, Kent. Detail of Norman moulding including chevron and cable.

13C   Norman ornament. Blind arcading. Canterbury Cathedral.

13D   Norman ornament: (above) billet and lozenge; (above right) two examples of billet ornament.

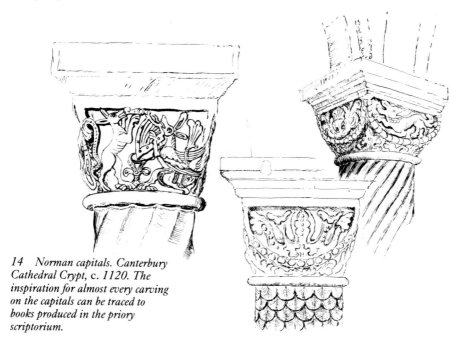

14   Norman capitals. Canterbury Cathedral Crypt, c. 1120. The inspiration for almost every carving on the capitals can be traced to books produced in the priory scriptorium.

decoration or, as in the west door of Rochester Cathedral
and at Barfreston, a Christ in Majesty set in an oval
mandorla recalling tympanum decoration in Aquitaine.
Another favourite form of Norman decoration used
externally as well as internally was blind arcading in the form
of linked or intersected arches often found below the main
window level. This was, as already mentioned, found across
the walls of towers in two or more tiers.

Apart from castles there is little substantial domestic
architecture left from this period. Two stone houses owned
by the Jewish community survive at Lincoln as well as the
ruins of a stone house at Christchurch in Dorset, and the
manor house at Boothby Pagnell near Grantham is the best
almost unaltered example. It consists of two floors, the lower
for storage, and the upper forming a hall with a fireplace,
with access direct from an external staircase. Unfortunately
the famous Jew's House on Steep Hill, Lincoln of about
1170 has had its façade considerably mutilated by the
introduction of a later shopfront. A number of stone houses
of considerable grandeur from this period are known to have
existed in Canterbury and London, but no trace of these
remain above ground.

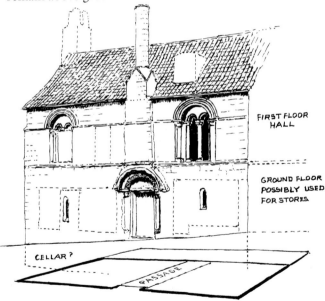

FIRST FLOOR
HALL

GROUND FLOOR
POSSIBLY USED
FOR STORES

CELLAR ?

PASSAGE

*15   Jew's House, Lincoln,
c. 1170-80, showing conjectural
appearance before alterations.
Dotted lines show later shop front
and windows. The chimney is taken
from Boothby Pagnell Manor
House, c. 1200.*

III

Early Gothic in England 1175-1290

The Gothic style appeared in England towards the end of the twelfth century, having originated in France. The term 'Gothic' itself was invented in the sixteenth century as one of derision suggesting that the medieval style had deviated from classical truth and had been imposed on Europe by the Goths who overran much of the Roman Empire. In England it is divided into three main stages: Early English *c.* 1175-1290, Decorated 1290-1350 and Perpendicular including Tudor 1350-1550. These dates are only approximate and there were wide regional variations especially in the north of England. The main characteristic of the Gothic style is the pointed arch found in windows, doorways and the rib structure of stone vaults. There is also a greater awareness of the solutions to structural problems, especially the resistance to vault pressures by a system of buttresses, and the opening-out of wall surfaces with larger windows. The development of the pointed arch had considerable advantages for twelfth-century builders, especially in the matter of vaulting, which hitherto had to cover square bays if the inclination of the arches was to remain equal. With the pointed arch, ribs could be inclined to any pitch to cover a rectangular bay.

Whilst pointed arches are found at Cluny and Autun in Burgundy from about 1100, the Abbey of St Denis in Paris is generally considered to be the birthplace of the style in about 1130. Over the next seventy years the style developed in France under the impetus of the great cathedral-building campaign and the monastic expansion of the then recently founded Cistercian order. Unfortunately the earliest examples of the style in England have been largely destroyed, such as Tynemouth Priory, Whitby Abbey and Fountains Abbey in Yorkshire. Fountains is perhaps the most beautiful ruin in England and shows admirably a mixture of Romanesque and Early Gothic features such as round and pointed arches. Whilst the side aisles have tunnel vaults the nave and choir were covered by a wooden roof perhaps similar to that found over the nave of Peterborough. In France all major churches were stone-vaulted, and Sens

Cathedral, completed about 1170 with sexpartite vaulting, might be seen as the best comparison with Fountains. Only after the disastrous fire in Canterbury Cathedral choir in 1174 was vaulting adopted for all major English cathedrals.

Some will claim Canterbury as the first English Gothic cathedral though only the choir and eastern Trinity Chapel were rebuilt, and that in the Transitional style between 1175 and 1190. It introduces lancet arches alongside semi-circular-headed arches adorned with chevron moulding. The vaulting is sexpartite following the pattern of Sens from where William, the master mason of Canterbury, came. Another stylistic link with Sens is the introduction of paired shafts and Corinthian capitals (see page 82).

Wells Cathedral, begun in 1186, owes nothing to a previously existing plan and may claim to exemplify the early adoption of Early English Gothic. The plan is cruciform terminating in a rectangular east end. The internal elevation is relatively low with a strong horizontal triforium division of continuous lancets between lower arcade and clerestory. Unlike contemporary French cathedrals there is no vertical shafting from the pavement to the springing of the vault at clerestory level acting as a bay division. The vault pattern in the nave is quadripartite, although the choir vault was

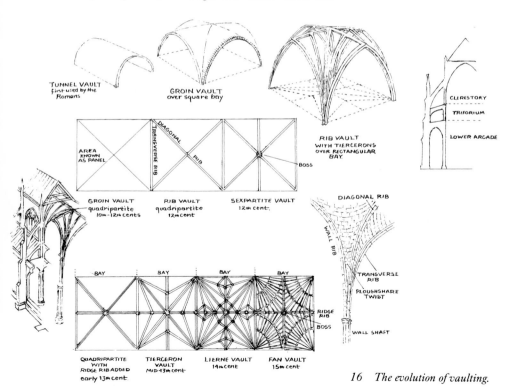

16   *The evolution of vaulting.*

altered to a more complex lierne pattern in the early fourteenth century. The undoubted glory of Wells is the west front, which acts as a giant sculptural screen extending to include the western towers as well. The nave is defined by three tall lancet windows beneath a tier of niches filled by the twelve apostles. Unlike French cathedrals of this period there is no projecting gabled porch; indeed the western entrance is visually insignificant compared with the boldly projecting vertical buttresses which define the nave, aisles, and flanking towers whose upper stages were only completed between 1367 and 1424.

Whilst Wells displays the lancet stage of early Gothic admirably, Lincoln Cathedral shows the continuous process of architectural development from the first stage of rebuilding in 1192 of the eastern transepts to the completion of the so-called Angel Choir in 1280. The nave, completed in the 1230s, displays triple lancets in the clerestory, but unlike Wells there are thin triple shafts rising from the lower arcade to divide the wall into bays. The triforium consists of two major arches in each bay with subsidiary openings beneath the plate pierced by a quatrefoil pattern. The nave piers of Lincoln limestone are dressed with slender shafts of Purbeck marble divided into two by annulets or rings of stone. The capitals display stiff-leaf foliage and are surmounted by circular abaci.

The nave vault shows an advance on the quadripartite pattern of Wells, with the introduction of a ridge rib and additional diagonals known as tiercerons. These help to lessen the weight of stone in each bay and direct the stress down into the bay shafts and arcade piers. A further counterbalance to the vault pressure against the clerestory walls was provided by flying buttresses. Further east beyond the crossing tower, which collapsed in about 1237, is what has been described by Sir Nikolaus Pevsner as the 'crazy vault' where the diagonal ribs manage to miss the middle of each bay so creating a lopsided effect.

During the early thirteenth century French builders were making advances in window design. From the simple plate tracery windows found at Chartres where the spandrels of each arch are pierced by a roundel, the masons of Reims a little later created the geometrical window where the whole arch is opened out into tall lancets and roundels formed by sections or 'bars' of stone. This window development spread to England before 1250. It was adopted for all kinds of ecclesiastical building and is admirably seen in the Angel Choir at Lincoln which although inspired by Ely Cathedral presbytery shows a considerable architectural advance. This great extension of five bays was built to house the shrine of St Hugh of Avalon, the instigator of the great rebuilding after the partial destruction of the Romanesque cathedral in

1185. This extension involved the demolition of the apsidal ending of the early Gothic choir. The Angel Choir is rich in carved decoration, and also stresses the combination of limestone and marble shafting to maximum advantage. The aisle windows are made up of combinations of three lancets and roundels whilst the east window consists of a yet greater permutation of lancets and roundels filling the complete space from wall to wall and up to the curvature of the vault.

The Angel Choir takes its name from the carved angels in the spandrels of the triforium arcade. The whole feeling of the design of this end of the cathedral points the way to the greater freedom of carved decoration to be found over the next hundred years. Notable decorative features here include dog-tooth ornament round the outermost moulding of each arch of the lower arcade, and leaf crockets sprouting between the marble shafts in the triforium, and the jambs of the east window. The clerestory is notable for the minor stone tracery copying that of the windows themselves. The vault is of simple tierceron pattern with the ridge rib emphasizing the length of the interior.

Most English cathedrals show a pattern of architectural development and change over several centuries; even Lincoln has a fourteenth-century crossing tower and extensions to the western Norman towers displaying a successful merging of late Gothic detail. Salisbury on the other hand was built – with the exception of the upper stage of the central tower and the spire – wholly in the Early English style, adhering to the lancet arch throughout. Started in 1220 to replace the cathedral of nearby Old Sarum it was completed in 1265. The plan, like those of Lincoln and Canterbury, has eastern transepts, but the long nave of ten bays ends like Wells in a west front which is really a large sculptural screen flanked by spirelets instead of square corner towers. The central bay of the façade displays the earliest gabled entrance porch to a cathedral after the French fashion, although less spectacular than, say, Laon, Reims or Bourges. Its west front has a number of stylistic features in common with Wells. The interior has unfortunately been over-restored by James Wyatt involving the destruction of a number of tombs and therefore looks somewhat cold. However the nave, like that of Wells, has a strong horizontal progression due to the absence of vertical shapes dividing arched bays. Although just a few years later than the nave of Lincoln, the vaulting is simpler following the quadripartite plan without a ridge rib.

Typical of this Early English interior is the extensive use of Purbeck marble, which is used for the slender detached shafts with roll-moulded capitals in the eastern Holy Trinity Chapel, started in 1220. In the nave each circular pier has four detached shafts divided by annulets. Although

RHEIMS 1254-90

CLERESTORY

TRIFORIUM

NAVE ARCADE

N. AISLE   NAVE   S. AISLE

17   Salisbury Cathedral: West Front, 1258-66. This front is virtually a stone screen built across the western termination of the nave and side aisles. Since the main entrance was under the North Porch the western entry is through inconspicuous doors beneath slightly projected gables. From the sketch of Reims we can see how much more emphasis was given to the western portals in French cathedrals. The lancet windows above the nave vault allows light into the roof for necessary repairs.

Salisbury was a cathedral of secular canons, it has like Wells and Lincoln several monastic features including the oldest surviving complete cloister of an English cathedral, completed in 1284 in the Decorated style, and an octagonal chapter house which is modelled very closely on that of Westminster Abbey.

It is generally acknowledged that English Gothic development in the twelfth and thirteenth centuries is about thirty years behind that of France. Apart from Canterbury choir partly rebuilt under the direction of William of Sens the other early Gothic examples mentioned were English interpretations of French Gothic principles, and this could also apply to the early twelfth-century work on the cathedrals of Worcester and York. A building which may be said to come closer to the spirit of French Gothic than its contemporaries, as well as marking the transition to the Decorated, is Westminster Abbey. As already mentioned this early medieval abbey was built under the direction of Edward the Confessor and consecrated in 1065. Highly impressed by the grandeur of the French coronation church of Reims, Henry II sought permission from the Pope to rebuild the abbey church. Permission was granted on condition that the Crown paid for the rebuilding and no financial burden was put on the Benedictine monks or pilgrims visiting the shrine of St Edward.

Work on building the eastern limb containing the presbytery, high altar, shrine and chevet termination of radiating chapels (similar in plan to Reims and Amiens) was

18   Westminster Abbey. Main building phases, and layout of monastic buildings.
A charter of King Edgar (957-75) refers to an existing church with ruined chapels. This was rebuilt by Edward the Confessor (1050-65) along with the monastic layout. In about 1245 Henry III began the rebuilding of the abbey church in the Early English style. Due to lack of sufficient money work came to a halt in 1259, and was not continued until 1376 with work on the nave. Henry Yevele, the master mason continued the work in the earlier Gothic style. Only the west window exhibits the true characteristics of the Perpendicular style. The disposition of the various monastic buildings follows that laid down in the plan of St Gall, c. 820.

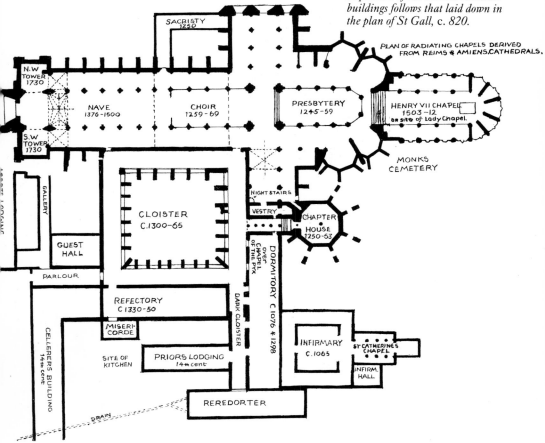

begun in 1245, and completed by 1260, a remarkably short time in view of the necessary demolition of the Romanesque work. The elevation is of three stages with a much-reduced triforium in keeping with French trends. Slender shafts of Purbeck marble divide each bay and provide a strong vertical accent up to the springing of the vault which contains a ridge and tierceron ribs. The richness of this royal foundation can be felt in the design of stamped panels with a leaf motif across the spandrels of the arches. The clerestory window tracery introduces the geometrical pattern of bar tracery similar to that of Reims dating from the 1230s. Unfortunately even though this was a royal rebuilding, money ran out in 1269 when only four bays west of the crossing were completed, and work came to a standstill for about a century, by which time the Gothic style in England had made radical advances.

IV

The later Gothic styles in England 1290-1530

By the late thirteenth century the Gothic style in England was attaining greater virtuosity as more daring building ventures were undertaken, coupled with a seemingly unlimited variety of carved decoration. This has led to the period between about 1290 and 1350 being designated the 'Decorated'. Apart from the rebuilding of Exeter Cathedral it was essentially an age of consolidation and embellishment; this also applies to parish churches, of which, apart from Heckington, Lincolnshire, and Patrington, Yorkshire, there are few examples exhibiting the Decorated style exclusively.

Just as Salisbury might be said to display the main characteristics of Early English, so Exeter might represent the Decorated. The Norman cathedral dating from shortly after 1100 was seen by Bishop Walter Bronescombe, who was present at the consecration of Salisbury in 1258, as being old-fashioned and lacking the dignity of the Early English style. He inaugurated the massive rebuilding which started in 1270-80 at the east end with the Lady Chapel. This was followed by a gradual westward progression which managed to retain two Norman towers as north and south transepts pierced with Decorated Gothic windows. It is the nave, under construction from 1328, which gives Exeter its special character. Standing against the west wall one can liken the receding bays of the nave with the sprouting tierceron ribs of the vault to an avenue of trees. The vault pattern is simple and repetitive as our eyes are drawn eastwards along the longest unbroken stretch of Gothic vaulting in Europe – it continues over the presbytery as well.

The nave of Exeter shows the further diminishing of the triforium which becomes nothing more than an arcaded screen with enlarged clerestory windows above. The decorative highlight of the nave is the Minstrels' Gallery projecting from the triforium on the north side. Its purpose was to hold a choir on Palm Sunday to sing antiphons and it is decorated with niches containing twelve angels playing musical instruments. The piers and arches of the lower arcade also attract attention. Unlike the typical Early English interior with piers and detached shafts, here the nave and presbytery arcade piers are diamond shaped in plan with alternate thick and thin shafts like pipes rising to subtle moulded capitals like inverted bells. The arches of the arcade are less acutely pointed than hitherto and are heavily moulded with numerous narrow bands and recesses.

Window tracery is perhaps the most easily distinguishable feature in the development of the Gothic style, and whilst simple geometrical tracery patterns are still found throughout this period, the west front of Exeter under construction between about 1330 and 1375 shows the quintessence of the style with the large 'flamboyant' traceried window. The pattern is dominated by a large circle in which there are twelve quatrefoil roundels which in turn support a five-pointed star. Beneath the circle on either side of the central light are two compartments beneath ogee curved tracery. These in turn are broken up into smaller compartments by curved tracery which conveys the impression from a distance of the window having been moulded in plastic. The west front extends as a screen over the side aisles with sloping battlemented wings in place of side towers to hide the flying buttresses behind; only the west front of Milan *c.* 1450-1500 bears any resemblance in this respect. As at Salisbury and Wells the west doors seem relatively unimportant in the wide sculptural screen in which they are set.

York Minster boasts much in the Decorated style. The rebuilding of the Norman church began in about 1225 with

19   Exeter Cathedral: West Front, 1346-75. As at Salisbury the buttressing against the nave is hidden by a screen of masonry instead of western towers flanking the Front. The western portal is relatively insignificant and is overwhelmed by the tiers of figure sculpture. The central gable contains a flamboyant traceried window above the vault level, to light the roof-timber area.

N.AISLE.   NAVE   S.AISLE

20   Exeter Cathedral. Decorated-style nave, fourteenth century. The north and south Norman towers were retained and incorporated into the transeptal division between nave and choir.

the south and then north transepts with an elaborate array of lancet windows. The transition can be seen in the octagonal chapter house begun in 1286. Unlike those of Westminster and Salisbury this is without a central pier as the vault, like a star in plan, is of wood and therefore does not exert as much pressure against the walls which are pierced by large windows fully spanning each bay. The tracery here is still geometrical. The early fourteenth-century nave of York is spacious and French in feeling with shafts rising unbroken from the base of each arcade pier to the springing of the vault, which is also of wood. Now the lower arcade is virtually half the total height of the elevation and the triforium is all but eliminated, becoming no more than a band of gabled niches between verticals forming the mullions of the clerestory windows above. The vault pattern introduces short diagonal lierne ribs (Fr. *lien* = tie) which link the transverse and tierceron ribs to the central ridge rib. Perhaps the crowning glory of the Minster is the west front flanked by tall pinnacled towers and boldly projecting buttresses which have almost the visual strength of Reims or Amiens. The west window is a fine example of curvilinear tracery which seems to writhe like a climbing plant, breaking it up into small glazed areas reminiscent of leaves.

Whilst the nave of Ely is Norman, the crossing and choir immediately to the east were reconstructed after the collapse of the central tower in 1322. The choir makes a most satisfactory join with the presbytery further to the east and has a flamboyant traceried triforium and clerestory. The vault is of the lierne variety. Instead of rebuilding the central tower on four major piers as before, these were demolished and the crossing was opened out into an octagon by building walls linking the last pier of each aisle bay. This and the octagonal lantern above were the creation of the cathedral sacrist, Alan of Walsingham. As at York, the vaulting of the octagon is of wood; it is crowned in the centre by a beautiful star vault and central boss representing Christ. The windows are of flamboyant tracery patterns as if to provide a final flourish before a return to sobriety. Faced on the outside in lead, this remarkable structure weighs over 400 tons and is delicately supported by a hidden frame of enormous oak beams.

Adjacent to the crossing at Ely on the north side is the Lady Chapel, 1321-49, a masterpiece of the Decorated style. Here, now sadly much mutilated, the walls beneath the windows are decorated with blind arcading surmounted by nodding ogee arches which terminate in pedestals for figure sculpture. The tracery of each arch is richly ornamented with crockets of naturalistic foliage. Between each ogee gable are small pinnacles. What figures remain have in many cases lost their heads but are still partly gilded. Traces of red and light blue paint also remain in the moulding of the arches.

Other cathedrals receiving extensions or embellishment at this time include Carlisle with a large flamboyant east window which may have inspired the west window at York. At Lichfield the most novel contribution to the cathedral is the eastern Lady Chapel from about the period 1320-36. It is aisleless, thus allowing for tall windows in each bay. Following continental models the east end is polygonal, and the chapel seems strongly under the influence of the Sainte-Chapelle, Paris, from the mid-thirteenth century. As at the contemporary Ely Lady Chapel the remaining wall space below the windows is filled with ogee-headed arcading. At Gloucester Cathedral we find on the tracery of the south nave aisle windows 'ball-flower' ornament, another characteristic of the Decorated style.

It was at one time assumed that the Perpendicular style followed the Decorated after the Black Death, 1350 being a suitable date for the division. However, the characteristics of the Perpendicular style are to be found at Gloucester Cathedral from about 1328, and some of them were clearly developed in St Stephen's Chapel of the Palace of Westminster dating from about 1300 and destroyed by fire in 1834. The Perpendicular or rectilinear style was practised for over two centuries and merges with the Tudor

21   Gloucester Cathedral Choir, 1337-50. This section through the choir shows the insertion of the Perpendicular 'cage' between Norman aisle and tribune. The height of the original clerestory is shown by dotted lines. The floor is shown cut away to reveal the crypt, 1089-1100.

and Elizabethan when it became overlaid with classical detail. The period was one of extensive building with hardly a major English cathedral escaping its influence; this applies also to parish churches, described later.

It is ironic that the style's most magnificent manifestation is also its earliest, namely the choir of Gloucester Cathedral, rebuilt 1337-50. The reason for the transformation of the Norman abbey church was the burial there in 1327 of the murdered King Edward II. Within a few years his tomb had become an object of veneration by countless pilgrims who also contributed substantially to the monastic funds. Strictly speaking the Norman choir was not demolished but rather 'shaved' to receive a rectilinear frame of vertical mullions and horizontal transoms covering the round arches of the lower arcade and triforium and culminating in an enlarged clerestory. Here as at Canterbury after the 1174 fire the reconstruction was governed by the remaining crypt beneath the choir and side aisles.

The east window vies with York for the distinction of being the largest Gothic window in Europe, some 72 feet high and 38 feet wide. It is actually wider than the choir proper as the easternmost bay walls are splayed to receive it. The basic tracery pattern is of simple rectilinear compartments without ogee curves. The mullions are of three thicknesses, and the window is clearly divided into three major compartments with two immensely thick mullions which branch out towards the top of the window. It was glazed in about 1350 in commemoration of the English victory at Crécy. The choir vault of stone is the most intricate lierne example in England with beautifully carved bosses, many representing a heavenly orchestra of angels.

To the north of the nave the closters were rebuilt from 1373 and now remain as the most complete example in Britain. It is here that we see the earliest appearance of fan vaulting which was later to be used so spectacularly at King's College Chapel, Bath Abbey and Peterborough and Canterbury Cathedrals. In the south walk there are twenty stone carrels or cells in which the monks sat at their studies, whilst in the north walk the lavatorium or washing place remains with its long stone water trough. On the cloister wall opposite there is a recess with iron rails to hold the monks' towels.

Another largely Norman-built cathedral which underwent extensive alteration during the fourteenth century is Winchester. First the choir was rebuilt from about 1320 with the present clerestory and wooden lierne vault completed in about 1500. More outstanding, though, was the encasing of the Norman nave in a Perpendicular-style dressing. Here the master mason William Wynford demolished the arches of the lower arcade and triforium. He then inserted pointed arches raised to the level of the previous triforium. These support a narrow gallery immediately below the clerestory, which is basically the Norman windows enlarged to a point and filled with Perpendicular tracery. As a result of the fourteenth-century dressing the piers are immensely thick, and as at York there is a shaft rising unbroken from the base of each pier to the springing of the lierne-patterned vault, level with the base of the clerestory windows. The west front is comparatively plain with a stress on the vertical provided by the large window and carried on up into the nave roof gable with blind tracery so characteristic of this period. There are western porches projecting well forward of the nave and aisle doors, but unlike in France no attempt is made to embellish them with rows of figure sculpture.

The inspiration behind the dramatic nave alterations at

22   Canterbury Cathedral.
Crossing tower known as 'Bell
Harry' c. 1480-1506.
Transitional clerestory c. 1180 on
right.

Winchester may be partly attributed to the decision of Archbishop Simon of Sudbury in 1378 to rebuild the Norman nave at Canterbury. For this task King Richard II's master mason Henry Yevele was appointed. Although the Norman piers supporting the central tower were retained those of the nave were demolished to foundation level. Within two building constraints, i.e. the requirement to construct the new piers and outer walls on the Norman foundations (as Yevele did with the nave of Westminister Abbey) and for the maximum height to be no more than the twelfth-century choir, he created one of the noblest masterpieces of late Gothic in Europe. With tall side aisles the arcade piers seem to soar upwards to meet the springing of the lierne vault at clerestory level. Against each pier the shafts are broken in their ascent by annulets which provide a pleasing break to their vertical lines. As at Winchester the triforium is no more than a blind stage between the lower arcade and clerestory.

Work at Canterbury went on throughout the fifteenth century and included the rebuilding of the south-west tower, the central transepts, and from the 1480s the crossing tower known as Bell Harry. This was a period of great tower building. Central towers rebuilt in this style include those of York, Durham, Gloucester and Canterbury. It is obviously a matter of personal taste as to which is the finest. For some, York seems rather squat being a lantern tower of one stage. That of Durham is of two stages with the openings of the lower narrower than those of the upper. The tower of Gloucester from after 1450 is beautifully divided into rectilinear compartments throughout its two stages. Its verticality is arrested by the half-way string course. The corners have diagonal buttresses diminishing to pinnacles just below parapet level. The summit has beautiful open-tracery pinnacles linked by 'open' battlemented parapets, a feature found elsewhere on church towers in Gloucestershire and Somerset.

At Canterbury work on the central tower to replace the 'Angel Steeple' progressed slowly and seems at first to have been intended as a single stage lantern tower. Only in the 1490s was it raised another fifty feet when master John Wastell of 'King's College, Cambridge' was consulted about its completion. It is built of 400,000 bricks and faced externally with strongly emphasized vertical strips broken by horizontal string courses. The lower stage windows are topped by ogee hoods and the division between this stage and the upper is marked by a lattice-work band. At each corner the pinnacles rise well above the open-traceried parapet and diminish in two gabled stages.

Besides large structural extensions to English cathedrals the Perpendicular period was one of extensive internal

23 *Gloucester Cathedral, central tower, c. 1450.*

furnishing. Stone choir screens (*pulpita*) and reredos behind altars were built, such as that at Winchester now restored after sixteenth-century mutilation. The century following the Black Death saw a considerable increase in chantry chapels and impressive tombs; many with lifelike sculptured effigies. Apart from royal tombs such as that of the Black Prince at Canterbury or Edward II at Gloucester, there are those of many ecclesiastics and noblemen who left vast memorials of their wealth and piety. Perhaps Winchester Cathedral and Tewkesbury Abbey have the finest remaining collection of chantry tombs outside Westminster. In both buildings these memorials take the form of tall rectangular enclosures of rectilinear tracery covered with a miniature stone vault. Usually there was sufficient space within the chapel for several persons to attend the Mass on the donor's anniversary or feast. The tomb was often in the form of a chest beneath the altar, or on one side of the chapel with a marble effigy. Occasionally, as on Archbishop Chichele's table tomb at Canterbury, there is a double effigy. One shows him in his earthly splendour dressed in his robes whilst beneath is a cadaver, a *memento mori*. At Tewkesbury Abbey there is a striking note of originality in the chantry of Edward, Lord Despenser, who died in 1375. Here he is placed beneath a canopied niche set in the middle of the roof of the fan-vaulted chapel; clad in armour he kneels facing the high altar in prayer.

A chantry foundation which can be said to mark the culmination of the development of the Perpendicular style is the magnificent Henry VII chapel at the east end of Westminster Abbey. Dedicated to Our Lady it was intended originally to be a shrine for the king's uncle Henry VI, whom it was hoped the Pope would canonize. The monks of Westminster contributed £500 for the papal licence to translate the king's body from Windsor to Westminster, but the sum demanded by Julius II for the canonization was too great and so the body remained at Windsor. Instead the chapel became the chantry chapel of Henry VII and his queen, Elizabeth of York.

Work began in January 1502, the site of the old Lady Chapel having been cleared. The walls of the chapel are almost screens of glass broken only by the polygonal buttresses against the side aisles and eastern apsidal chapels. The curvature of the windows is of the Tudor four-centred type with the tracery reduced to the simplest rectilinear pattern which extends across the external remaining wall surfaces and buttresses. With royal funds available, some amassed from dissolved religious houses, the internal decoration could be lavish, especially that of the fan-and-pendant vaulting by William Vertue. Few examples of vaulting with projecting pendants exist apart from the choir of Christ Church Cathedral, and the Divinity School, both in Oxford, and St George's Chapel, Windsor.

Here in this fan-and-pendant vault the bay divisions are marked by transverse arches decorated with tracery like fine teeth which seem to disappear behind conoids tapering to delicate pendants as the numerous ribs come together. The conoids meet at the ridge of the vault which is interrupted at intervals by secondary pendants, a design simplified in the wooden ceiling of Hampton Court Chapel from about 1530. Indeed, the pendant as a projection on vaulting develops from the hammer-beam roof construction.

It is the tomb of Henry VII and his queen hidden behind its high protective grill which heralds England's belated introduction to Renaissance ornament. In 1512 the Florentine sculptor Pietro Torrigiano was contracted to make the tomb and the two effigies in bronze. The sides are adorned with circular wreaths divided by highly ornamental pilaster strips topped with Corinthian capitals. At the corners of the tomb sit small angels, beautifully three-dimensional, acting as mourners for the deceased.

The Gothic style was to remain throughout the sixteenth century, but gradually losing its grip as the effects of the Renaissance were felt. The English Reformation and dissolution of the monasteries ended major church building for at least a century; Bath Abbey, rebuilt 1500-39, was the last major church to be consecrated before the first act for the dissolution and confiscation of church property in 1536. It exhibits the purest forms of rectilinear design even in the fan vaulting. Several years before the rebuilding of the Abbey was completed, Italian craftsmen were imported to Cambridge to carve the magnificent screen in King's College Chapel. Here we find panel divisions of semi-circular arches flanked by Renaissance mannerist pilasters yet harmonizing with the majestic Gothic interior. Perhaps if we seek hard enough, though, we can see that the Gothic never really died in England. Throughout the seventeenth century it was to be used for example at Oxford, in the hands of England's greatest Classical architect, Wren, who designed the Gothic Tom Tower at Christ Church.

V

Medieval parish churches from the Norman to the Tudor period

England is fortunate in the number of medieval churches which still survive, as these reflect more closely than cathedrals and abbeys the economic and social conditions of a particular area. The use of ornament is often more individual, perhaps unique to a small district, and unlike in the greater churches, the building material is frequently taken from the immediate locality. For example, whilst Canterbury Cathedral is largely of imported Caen stone, the parish churches of East Kent are mostly of flint with Kentish ragstone used for window tracery, door jambs and the dressing of buttresses and parapets. They vary enormously in scale and complexity, from the simple two-cell Norman examples of Adel, Yorkshire, or Hales, Norfolk to the grandeur of St Mary Redcliffe, Bristol. Some never grew beyond their eleventh- or early twelfth-century simple layout, whilst others, especially in the more wealthy parts of the country, were extensively rebuilt during the later Middle Ages with the profits from the wool trade with Flanders, or bequests to create perpetual chantries for the nobility. Very few examples contain two or more styles in equal measure; in most one or two predominate. A church might have been built in the Norman period and have received extensive alterations only during the Perpendicular, such as the rebuilding of the chancel. Others were totally rebuilt during the Decorated and Perpendicular periods, such as the great 'wool' church of Lavenham, Suffolk. As we have seen the Decorated period was one of embellishment rather than extensive building, so there are few examples of churches built in the Decorated period apart from Heckington, Lincs and Patrington, Yorks.

In order to gain a picture of parish church development throughout the Middle Ages it is best first to look at general features of planning. It must however be borne in mind that there were sometimes exceptional factors governing the plan, not least monastic requirements in cases where there was dual use, the parishioners sometimes being confined to an aisle. At Manchester, where the church was served by secular canons, the whole nave was used by the people of the parish. See drawing 12, pp. 22-3.

Before the beginning of the twelfth century church-building in stone was mostly limited to abbeys and cathedrals and many Saxon structures remained in use until, as the monk historian Ordericus Vitalis said, the 'houses and temples' that had been built by Edgar and Edward and other Christian kings were pulled down and replaced by others of greater size and elegance. The plan at first adopted by the Norman builders was the simple two-cell, that is a nave and chancel divided by a chancel arch. Chancels could be either apsidal or rectangular, the former predominating in the southern counties. An excellent

24 *Medieval window development, Norman to Tudor.*

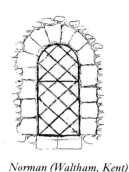

Norman (Waltham, Kent)

Norman exterior (Fordwich, Kent)

Early English Lancets (Hastingleigh, Kent)

Norman (Canterbury Cathedral)

Early English, geometrical (Ovingdean, Sussex)

Decorated, curvilinear (Chilham, Kent)   *Decorated, curvilinear (Hastingleigh, Kent)*

Decorated, reticulated (St Denys, York)

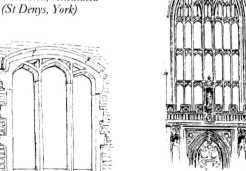

Perpendicular (Lavenham, Suffolk)

Tudor (St Dunstan's, Canterbury)

Perpendicular (Bath Abbey)

example of a church from about 1100 with virtually no alteration is Barfreston near Canterbury; the east end is decorated with round-headed blind arcading and a wheel window in the roof gable. On the southern side of the nave is the doorway set beneath a tympanum. Sometimes a tower was introduced between the nave and chancel as at Stewkley, Bucks, or a low bellcote above the western gable as at Adel. The central tower plan might also have north and south transepts so creating a cruciform layout as at Hemel Hempstead, Herts.

Assuming we follow the usual progress of development, we might find the first real extensions to a parish church occurring in the middle of the twelfth century with the construction of, first, a north nave aisle, to be followed by one on the south. A rare late Norman plan is the circular nave model derived from the Knightly Orders of which only five examples now remain. The best is the Holy Sepulchre Church in Cambridge which was joined to a small eastern chancel, rebuilt in the fifteenth and nineteenth centuries. Another, in the style transitional from Norman to Early Gothic is the Temple Church in London joined to a 'hall-church' choir modelled closely on the Holy Trinity Chapel at the east end of Salisbury Cathedral.

The Early English style is characterized most forcefully by lancet windows and dog-tooth moulding which supplants the Norman chevron. Three churches which demonstrate the simplicity and visual appeal of lancet arches are Ketton, Darlington and Uffington. The last has an unaisled cruciform plan with a unique octagonal crossing tower. The lancets at Uffington are in pairs in the chancel, but triple set in the east wall and transepts. When there are three arches, the centre arch is raised above its two neighbours. Where side aisles have been introduced, the arcade of pointed arches between main and side aisles is raised on piers slightly more slender than hitherto. In the more spectacular churches of this period such as West Walton, Norfolk, the main circular piers have detached shafts with dividing annulets. At Stone, Kent, the nave arcade is taller and has four thin shafts of marble attached to each pier, producing what is known as a compound pier. Most capitals were moulded in the form of an inverted bell between a circular abacus and a neck resting on the shafts below. Where decoration occurs it is usually in the form of stiff-leaf foliage, or a simple water-leaf form. Within the curvature of arches thin bands of dog tooth often appear.

As in cathedrals, windows were gradually transformed from the simple lancet through the plate tracery stage, to the geometrical bar tracery variety. Windows were, however, still generally small in the absence of the strong buttressing of later periods.

Towers with spires were now found especially in the Midland countries, where the broach variety was favoured. The towers, if new, were usually erected at the western end of the nave, even as a detached structure to allow for the future lengthening of the nave. They were usually of two stages, the upper for the bells. The spires were octagonal, thus creating an awkward junction at the four corners of the tower. This was overcome by the introduction of broaches, a form of split pyramid which filled the space and created a satisfying visual link between the corners and diagonal sides of the spire. At intervals the spires were pierced with lucarne openings traceried like small windows. An excellent example is Ketton. A southern variety of spire found especially in Kent, Surrey and Sussex is the splay-foot which is also found in the Rhineland. Excellent examples, both in Kent, are Hinxhill and Fordwich.

Few parish churches date purely from the Decorated period; perhaps the finest are Heckington, Lincs and Patrington, Yorks, which have already been mentioned. With the further development of window tracery walls were now pierced with larger windows, and chancels might be lit by an east window filling most of the available wall space including the gable area. The confidence to open out such wide areas of wall was brought about by the increased understanding of buttressing and wall supports. Side aisles on both sides of the nave are more frequent and have a porch projecting on the south. Where western towers were built they joined the nave and were sometimes of considerable height, necessitating boldly projecting corner

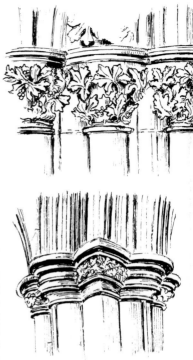

26 Decorated-style ornament: foliated capitals, Southwell Minster, Notts. (top), York Minster (above); four-leaf flower ornament (below), and ball-flower (bottom).

25A York, Holy Trinity. Thirteenth-century doorway detail showing dog-tooth moulding.

25B West Walton, Norfolk. Early English stiff-leaf capital with detached shafts, thirteenth century.

27A   Ketton, Leics: a fine example of the Early English style showing lancet windows and a broach spire.

27B   Fordwich, Kent. Overlapping shingle spire, thirteenth century.

buttresses. Spires were now set back behind parapets, and at the four corners tall pinnacles replaced the broach of the previous style.

After the beginning of the fourteenth century additions such as vestries, Lady Chapels and chantries were grafted on to the sides of naves and chancels. Besides the window tracery other characteristic features of this period include the piercing of buttresses with ogee gable niches, and pinnacles sprouting numerous crockets and terminated with a foliated finial. As with spires, so roofs were also set back behind a parapet often decorated with open 'curvilinear' tracery as on Heckington chancel.

As the name of the style suggests this was a period of lavish adornment, and it was in the fourteenth century that the craft of the stone-carver reached its greatest naturalism. Capitals are frequently dressed with heavily undercut leaves which seem to grow out of the stone. Leaves copy known species even to the veins: oak, chestnut, sycamore and vine were popular, and excellent examples of capitals exist at Patrington, Heckington and Great Missenden in Bucks. At St Mary Redcliffe, Bristol, the north porch entrance is adorned with a triple band surround of foliated ornament in which miniature figures and birds lose themselves in the riot of decoration.

Most interiors were covered by open-timber roofs, but vaulting occasionally appears in aisles or side chapels. Patrington is a fine example where the aisles are vaulted, probably by masons from York Minster. The carving of the nave capitals and arch moulding here is similar to York. Other frequently found ornaments include the ball-flower in window and door jambs, and the four-leaf flower.

After the economic recovery from the Black Death, which swept England in 1349-50, there was the final and greatest era of church-building before the Reformation. Although the Perpendicular may seem dull to some after the exuberance and virtuosity of the previous style, many magnificent alterations and additions were made to parish churches, such as the rebuilding of naves or chancels, the completion of towers and adding of chantry chapels, which in the case of Witney, Oxon, greatly alter the basic ground plan from that of a simple cruciform. Some reached cathedral proportions such as St Mary Redcliffe; Newark, Notts; Wakefield, Yorks; and St Michael, Coventry. Where a virtual rebuilding took place the church might resemble a vast aisled hall from end to end, as does St Nicholas, King's Lynn. This type of open planning was favoured by the Dominicans and Franciscans, who placed emphasis on preaching to large lay congregations.

Whilst all English counties can boast a fair number of Perpendicular churches, the finest examples are in the 'woollen' counties of the Midlands, East Anglia and South Yorkshire. Perhaps those of Suffolk, such as Long Melford and Lavenham, have the most typical stylistic characteristics. The former is nine bays in length, flanked by aisles, and with no structural division between the nave and chancel. At the east end of the north aisle is the chantry chapel of John Clopton, Sheriff of Norfolk and Suffolk, whose benefaction was largely responsible for the rebuilding of the church. He also provided for the building of the eastern Lady Chapel which is also aisled. This was the last part of the church to be built from about 1496 apart from the western tower, only completed in the twentieth century.

A major new feature in parish churches from the mid-fourteenth century is the clerestory, and this is admirably seen at Long Melford, creating almost the effect of a glass screen. Suffolk does not have building stone readily available, so to cut down the cost of transport flint is used extensively for wall facing. At Lavenham and Long Melford there are delicate flush-work patterns in flint and stone between the clerestory windows and in the battlemented parapet above, simulating blind tracery. Roof pitches now decrease dramatically, thus inviting the extensive use of open traceried parapets providing a delicate silhouette

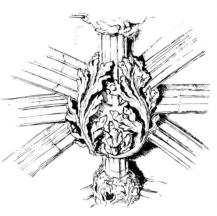

28 Decorated style ornament. Beverley Minster, Yorks. Vault bosses from the mid-fourteenth century.

against the sky, as at Lavenham.

Spires were still built but in lesser numbers although some were of extreme height even by Continental standards as at Louth, Lincs, and St Michael, Coventry, and of considerable embellishment. Suffolk and Norfolk churches usually had flint towers with stone dressing for the buttresses and windows. Lavenham tower has a fine stone parapet displaying blind lattice-work tracery on the south and north sides. In Suffolk there are still over 40 early medieval round towers. They sometimes received an additional octagonal belfry in the fifteenth century. These were of the utmost simplicity as at Mutford, which is topped by flushwork battlementing. In the stone belt counties towers are extremely impressive, with stages of rectilinear blind panelling sometimes continuing the verticality set by the mullions of the window and belfry openings. Outstanding is the tower of St Botoph, Boston, Lincs, which is surmounted by an octagonal lantern stage in which a lamp was hung at night to guide mariners entering the river Witham from the Wash. A similar lantern stage surmounts the tower of All Saints' Pavement, York, which acted as a beacon for travellers on their way through the forest of Galtres to the city. Towers in Gloucestershire and Somerset were often topped by an elaborate open-traceried parapet, with exceedingly tall corner pinnacles also opened into rectilinear compartments. That of St Mary, Taunton, is similar to the crossing tower of Gloucester Cathedral. At St Stephen's, Bristol, the pinnacles have open-traceried wings projecting from each corner and supported by a boldly overhanging cornice beneath. Crossing towers are not of such height as western towers due frequently to their having

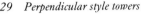

29   Perpendicular style towers

Taunton, Somerset. A fine example of a late Perpendicular tower with open tracery parapet and pinnacles similar to Gloucester Cathedral central tower.

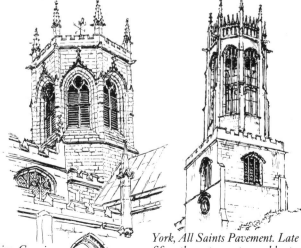

Nantwich, Cheshire. Crossing Tower, fifteenth-century

York, All Saints Pavement. Late fifteenth-century octagonal lantern similar to that of Boston, Lincs.

been raised on the foundations and wall supports of earlier structures. St Mary's, Beverley, Yorks, has a fine central tower with a lower stage adorned with circular windows. Above the belfry stage is adorned with large slatted openings and a parapet displaying intermediate pinnacles on each side. At Nantwich, Cheshire, there is a rare fifteenth-century octagonal crossing tower.

Besides towers, a notable feature of many church exteriors was the porch, usually on the southern side. Often it was rebuilt during the Perpendicular period although the original aisle or nave doorway was retained. Far from being simply covered entries to the door some porches were of considerable projection and height. Cirencester, Glos., has the largest in England, three storeys in height with the upper floors used for the meeting of the various trade guilds. At nearby Northleach the south porch has an upper storey which was used for a grammar school. Many were decorated with an array of delicately canopied niches, but often due to their nearness to the ground, the statuary has been destroyed. Some of the Suffolk church porches exhibit extensive flushwork decoration.

With the large and often plainly glazed windows, interiors appear light, and with a clerestory, often quite high. Arcade piers are slender with shafts divided by shallow curved recesses. At Chipping Camden, Glos., the octagonal piers are concave and bear a distinct similarity to those of Annaberg in Saxony which is contemporary. Capitals may be decorated with foliage or simply form polygonal breaks to the shafts as at Lavenham. The space between the arcade

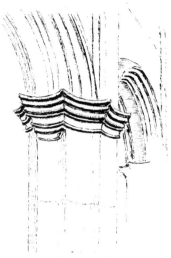

31   Perpendicular style capitals

Chipping Camden, Glos. Late fifteenth-century nave pier. The concave faces should be noticed.

Hastingleigh, Kent. Fifteenth-century pier.

30   Lavenham, Suffolk. Corner of Spring Chantry showing late fifteenth-century use of flush work. The lattice balustrade should also be noticed.

arches and the clerestory known as the spandrel might be decorated with blind tracery, foiled roundels, lattice work, or simply left plain. Arcade and window arches now tended to decrease their pitch almost to the state of losing their point thus returning to a semi-circle. The most characteristic arch is that known as the four-centred. After 1500 rectangular windows appear in clerestories and aisles with tracery of the simplest form of mullion divisions.

As clerestories were often introduced to the naves sometimes built several centuries earlier, the variety of timber roof found in the fifteenth and early sixteenth century embraced the full range of types found hitherto from the tie beam and barrel to the hammer beam – perhaps the most popular. At March, Cambs., the hammer beams are adorned with carved angels supporting shields. Only one medieval parish church in England was vaulted throughout, St Mary Redcliffe, Bristol, with a lierne type. At Cullompton, Devon, the Lane Aisle is fan vaulted to serve as a chantry chapel for John Lane, a wealthy clothier of the town. At St Mary's, Warwick, the chancel is roofed with a unique skeleton-rib vault – the ribs seeming to detach themselves from panels behind in the manner of flying ribs found in Eastern European Gothic.

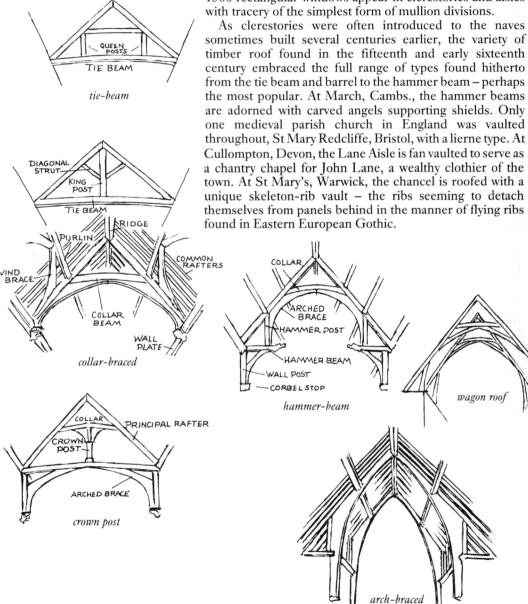

32   Medieval timber roof design.

VI

Medieval parish church furnishings

Few churches retain many of their medieval furnishings apart from fonts and stone pulpits. Clapton-in-Gordano, Somerset, is almost unique in retaining wooden seats of the fourteenth century. Wooden fittings were easily removed by iconoclasts if they exhibited religious decoration which did not accord with the views of the Reformers of the sixteenth century, or offended Puritan taste in the seventeenth. This extended to screens enclosing chantry chapels as well as rood screens beneath the chancel arch. Some excellent examples of the latter do, however, survive, though the roods are missing. The screen at Plymtree, Devon, not only has a riot of vine-leaf carving and lierne vaulting of wood beneath the gallery but also medieval painted figures in the lower panels depicting the nativity story. An equally impressive screen of wood survives at Flamborough, Yorks., although all the carved figures are missing. Choir stalls survive in a number of large churches to which a college of

33   Rood Screen, Flamborough, Yorks. Timber rood screen complete with loft. Fifteenth-century, against Norman chancel arch. The position of the Holy Rood, i.e. Cross, flanked by the Virgin Mary and St John, is shown.

priests was attached. Outstanding is Nantwich, and Manchester (now the Cathedral), although in a number of cases choir stalls were removed from monasteries at the Dissolution and sold to neighbouring parishes as at Whalley, Lancs.

Fonts were of stone and usually situated towards the west end of the nave or side aisle. They are frequently the oldest datable record of the foundation of a church, surviving repeated alteration or rebuilding; that at St Martin, Canterbury, may date from the early seventh century. Pre-thirteenth-century examples are often simple round drums with a roughly hewn basin in the centre. The carving, a mixture of banded pattern work and scriptural narrative, was of shallow relief, although late medieval fonts attain considerable grandeur. These were usually of two octagonal stages raised on one or more steps. The upper or bowl stage was divided into panels with quatrefoils and heraldic devices

34   Piscinas and sedilias

Waltham, Kent, piscina c. *1350.*

Waltham, Kent, sedilia c. *1350.*

Caistor, Northants, piscina, thirteenth-century and sedilia, late twelfth-century.

or, as frequently found in East Anglia, panels depicting the Seven Sacraments, and the Crucifixion.

A feature of great delicacy where they survive are font covers which often take the form of enormous octagonal pinnacled structures of wood raised by a rope on a pulley. An excellent example at Halifax, Yorks, reflects the window tracery of the period in its two main stages.

Depending on the wealth of the parish or the status of the church certain chancel furnishings might be adorned with highly intricate stone carving. On the right wall of a chancel (south) would be a piscina, a recess usually beneath a pointed arch containing a shallow stone basin with a drain for washing the sacred vessels. On the right of the piscina was the sedilia, a row of seats to be used by the priest, deacon and sub-deacon during Mass. In these can be found some of the finest achievements in the stone-carvers' art to rival the decoration at Southwell Minster Chapter House, and Ely Cathedral Lady Chapel. Perhaps the Ely craftsmen were responsible for the sedilia at Hawton, Notts, which has survived completely intact, as has the Easter Sepulchre used as the repository for the Blessed Sacrament from Good Friday to Easter Sunday. Easter Sepulchres were often tall wall structures of three stages: the lowest containing niches for figures of the sleeping soldiers, above it an arched recess for the Sacrament, and the top stage reserved for a statue of the risen Christ.

Many medieval church interiors may now appear to the visitor as being rather cold and lacking in colour. This may be due to the loss of medieval stained glass, although the Victorians in their zeal for restoration sometimes obliterated much-needed light by the introduction of strongly coloured glass. On the other hand walls were frequently painted with scenes from scripture to provide visual instruction for the unlettered. The most prominently painted area would be the wall above the chancel arch reserved for the Doom. The finest is in St Thomas's, Salisbury, where Christ sits on a double rainbow in accordance with the prophecy of the angels after the Ascension. On the left, the dead rise from the grave for the Last Judgement, whilst on the right the condemned are dragged down to Hell in chains. At Wenhaston, Suffolk, the Doom is painted in oils on wooden boards cut to fit the space over the chancel arch rather than, as usual, in tempera on dry plaster. Other popular subjects for wall paintings included the Crucifixion, Resurrection, St Christopher carrying the child, and St Michael, who sometimes appears with scales to fulfil his task of weighing souls. As already mentioned the panels of rood screens were often painted, as was the carved ornamentation on capitals and in arcades.

35 Nantwich, Cheshire. Ambo or stone pulpit, fifteenth-century.

36A Hastingleigh, Kent. Font, twelfth-century.

36B East Dereham, Norfolk. Font, fifteenth-century, depicting the Seven Sacraments.

VII

Medieval monastic planning

It is hard for us to visualize the size and grandeur of many medieval abbeys and priories since often little survives apart from a few sections of walling, or the recording of the existence of a once-proud foundation in the name of a modern thoroughfare such as Abbey Street or Almonry Gate. The visitor to Evesham, for instance, will find nothing of the former Benedictine abbey except a tower in a park. It was levelled to the ground and the stones re-used, as was often the case, for domestic building. At Fountains Abbey, stone was removed in the early seventeenth century for the building of the charming Jacobean-style Fountains Hall nearby. Sometimes the Court of Augmentations set up by Parliament with the passing of the first Act of Suppression

37   *The former Benedictine Priory of Durham showing remaining buildings.*

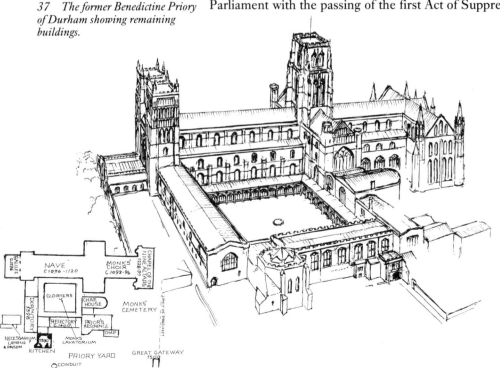

BAILEY C.1796
NAVE C.1096-1120
MONKS' CHOIR C.1093-96
CHAPEL OF THE NINE ALTARS 1228-37
CLOISTERS
DORMITORY 1398
CHAP. HOUSE
MONKS' CEMETERY
LIMIT OF PRECINCT
REFECTORY C.1400
PRIOR'S RESIDENCE
CHAP.
NECESSARIUM LATRINE & PRISON
1380
MONKS LAVATORIUM
KITCHEN
PRIORY YARD
GREAT GATEWAY 1500
CONDUIT

38   Chester Cathedral
Night Stairs, fourteenth-century,
leading from Dormitory to Cloister.
Upper quatrefoil window blocked
up by later vaulting of cloister.

39   Chester Cathedral
Entrance to Chapter House,
c. 1220. A fine example of Early
English rib vaulting.

in 1536 allowed the local townspeople to purchase the whole of a monastic church for their own worship. This happened most frequently with Benedictine foundations such as Great Malvern Priory, Malmesbury Abbey, and Tewkesbury where the townspeople paid the Crown £453 for the abbey church. Cistercian, Carthusian and Cluniac foundations out in the countryside were readily allowed to fall into ruin or act as a quarry for future builders. The most complete monastic remains in England are those of the Benedictine abbey of Chester, and in many cases buildings have been incorporated into schools founded in the former monastic precinct, as at Westminster and Christ Church, Canterbury.

Monastic planning tended to adopt a set formula first seen at St Gall in the ninth century, and which varied little throughout the Middle Ages. The church was at the centre of the monk's day and was planned for his purposes. Most were cruciform with a long nave and choir. In Benedictine foundations the community used the eastern half of the church from the crossing or last two bays of the nave. West of this point the nave was used for lay worship. Eight priories in England were also cathedrals from the mid-eleventh century. Cistercian monastic churches were wholly enclosed for the use of their brethren; however since the brethren in each house were divided into monks and lay-brothers, the nave was reserved for the latter who normally outnumbered the ordained community.

The cloister was usually on the south side of the nave because of the sun, although it was placed on the north when dictated by the monastic water system, pumped through pipes to the lavatorium within a cloister walk.

The main buildings were arranged round the cloister. On the east side would be the dormitory with direct access to the church via the Night Stairs, which still remain at Hexham Priory. Adjacent to the dormitory was the chapter house (Lat. *capitulum*, council) where the community gathered each day for business and prayers for the deceased brethren. Often it was octagonal with vaulting sprung from a central column as at Westminster which also retains its original medieval tiled floor and paintings on the walls. Another plan was the rectangular favoured by the Cistercians as at Fountains and Tintern. The rectangular chapter house at Canterbury (Christ Church) completed just before 1400 is the largest in England, about one hundred feet long and forty feet wide. It is crowned with a magnificent barrel ceiling of Irish bog-oak.

Much of the side opposite the nave was occupied by the refectory, kitchen and calefactorium or warming house. The refectory was the eating hall of the community. The abbot, prior and important guests would sit at the high table raised on a dais at one end of the hall. At one side of the hall would be a stone pulpit for the reading of scriptural texts or the lives of the saints during meals. The best preserved examples of monastic refectories are at Chester and Beaulieu, Hants (the latter now serves as the parish church). Kitchens were normally adjacent to the refectory but placed so that the smell of cooking would not reach the cloister. The great detached fourteenth-century kitchen at Durham survives in its entirety. The interior is octagonal with fireplaces in the angles. A similar plan survives at Glastonbury where the kitchen is the only substantial building remaining. The calefactorium was the monks' common room and the only place where a fire was normally allowed other than the kitchen. Here heat was provided by a brazier of charcoal.

The west side of the cloister was usually flanked by the cellarium, where the produce from the monastic estates was stored. At Fountains it takes the form of a magnificent three-hundred-foot-long vaulted undercroft above which was the lay-brothers' dormitory. The cellarer was an important monastic official and would therefore have his own quarters adjoining, whilst in the vicinity would also be the abbot's quarters, including guest rooms for distinguished visitors.

Due to the incorporation of a number of Benedictine houses as 'Cathedrals of the New Foundation' in 1541 their cloisters survive entire. Those of Gloucester have been mentioned earlier (p. 38), complete with glazed arcading, stone carrels and lavatorium. Often cloister walks were without glass or glazed only on one side; at Christ Church, Canterbury, holes remain in the jambs of the southern arcade into which iron glazing bars were set. Many cloister walks were vaulted and still amaze us with the complexity of rib patterns, and carved stone bosses providing a visual interpretation of the Old and New Testaments as seen at Norwich.

Adjacent to the dormitory was the necessarium or reredorter built over an undercroft through which the main drain or a river flushed running water. Plans were similar with rows of wooden seats separated from each other by a partition of wood or stone.

To the east of the cloister buildings would be the infirmary which at Christ Church, Canterbury, took the form of a large columned hall with aisles. At the eastern end was a chapel, and jutting out from the north aisle was a dining hall in which it was permitted to eat meat. An infirmary would be used for the sick brethren as well as those too old to follow the normal monastic rule of life. Near the infirmary would be the monks' cemetery, an ever-present reminder to the monk that he had taken vows at his solemn profession which were for the rest of his life.

Since a monastery was an independent community responsible for its own survival and not dependent on society at large, a monastic precinct would contain a number of ancillary buildings such as workshops, stables, granaries, a bakehouse and a brewery. Few of these survive, but at Canterbury (Christ Church) the bakehouse and brewhouse from about 1300 are now used by The King's School. Many Benedictine foundations housed shrines of saints which were a place of great pilgrimage. The most famous were Canterbury and Westminster and so a number of guest houses were erected to accommodate pilgrims.

Sometimes when little else survives of a once powerful

monastery the precinctal gatehouse alone remains as at
Bury St Edmund's. These often acted as lodgings for
visitors as well as the gatekeeper and were of considerable
size. The façade was frequently adorned with niches for
statuary including the patron saint of the foundation.
Complete gatehouses surviving include those at Durham, St
Albans, Ely, and in Canterbury, two from St Augustine's
Abbey, as well as the Tudor Christ Church gate from about
1515 – the last to be completed in England before the
Dissolution.

40   Durham Priory Gateway,
fifteenth-century.

41   Canterbury, Christ Church
Priory, Water Tower. Ground
storey c. 1150, upper c. 1390.

VIII

Late medieval castles and manor houses

As we have already seen, the Normans created an extensive system of stone fortifications to guard the coastline and major lines of communication in England. As with parish churches the Norman work often remains at the core of subsequent building admirably demonstrated in the Tower of London and Dover Castle. In both examples the proud donjon or keep stands above the network of surrounding walls. After the introduction of a stone keep usually raised on a motte (Lat. – *mota*) the wooden walls were replaced by those of stone to form two or more defended enclosures known as baileys, within which would be subsidiary buildings and an exercise ground for the garrison. Few castles survive entire and unaltered from this period, although perhaps Richard I's Château-Gaillard upon the Seine (*c.* 1190) conveys the best idea of such a plan. Variations of the motte-and-bailey plan were built throughout the Middle Ages, and in spite of a certain defensive weakness it was adopted by Edward I at Flint in the 1270s.

Since the object of a castle plan was defence, to hold the keep against any assailant, an elaborate system of mural

42   The architectural terminology of a castle.

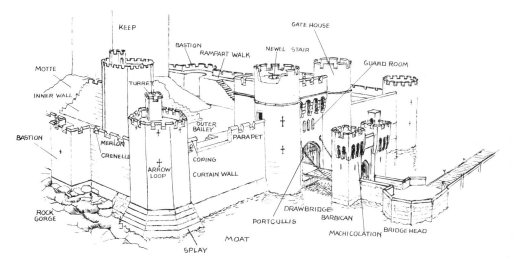

(Lat. – *murus*) or wall towers was introduced, inspired by
Roman and Byzantine fortifications. These were placed at
regular intervals, and with their additional height they
allowed each section of wall to be covered by adequate
firepower from bowmen on the ramparts. Towers also acted
as buttressing since there were obvious limits, including
financial, to the thickness of walls. A further form of
strength was created by the splaying of the base of mural
towers which impeded the tunneller as well as the assailant
with ladders. Projectiles dropped from the ramparts would
bounce out from the splay against any attacker. The earliest
towers used systematically were rectangular in plan and are
at Dover (see figure 8) and Framlingham, Suffolk, dating
from just before 1200.

Castle walls were of sufficient thickness to allow a walk-
way known as a rampart to encircle the castle. Access to this
was normally from the first or second storey of the mural
towers. Protection for the garrison guard was provided by a
high parapet pierced by gaps known as crenelles, the
remaining uprights known as merlons, forming the familiar
battlements or crenellation. Slit openings or embrasures in
walls were splayed on the inside to allow for the aiming of an
archer yet provide the maximum of protection against attack
from without.

In the thirteenth and fourteenth centuries particular
attention was paid to the fortification of a castle gateway
which by virtue of being an entrance could easily be the
weakest point in the defence system of the whole castle. At
Dover Henry II placed stone towers on either side of the
entrances to the inner bailey shortly before 1200. By the end
of the thirteenth century the flanking towers had become
rounded and the gateway developed into a gatehouse of
several storeys and considerable depth. Excellent examples
survive at Harlech and Saltwood, Kent.

Additional defensive protection provided in gatehouses
included a portcullis at each end of the passage, raised and
lowered in stone grooves from a chamber above. The ceiling
or vault of the passage was often pierced with 'meurtrières'
or 'murder holes' through which missiles could be dropped
on any enemy. Similar openings occur in the projecting
gallery or machicolation between the flanking towers.

The motte-and-bailey castle, impressive and spacious as
it might be, had one very serious weakness: if an assailant
managed to breach the wall system he could virtually starve
the garrison imprisoned in the keep into submission. The
late thirteenth century therefore saw the introduction of a
new plan in which the latest techniques of defence were
incorporated. Instead of having a two-piece system as
hitherto with a keep or donjon at its heart, the new plan was a
single system of close-knit interrelated defences adequately

defended by a tall wall enclosing a semi-quadrangular
space. The strength which had hitherto been reserved for
the keep was now disposed in the massive mural towers
which became huge circular drums, or polygonal with splays
or spurs at their base. Edward I's castles at Caernarfon and
Conway may be considered the finest examples, both
started in 1283. In effect the walls became tall triple-stage
firing platforms with two galleries worked into the space
beneath the ramparts.

Without the restrictions imposed by a keep the domestic
apartments could be spaciously laid out behind the
protecting walls including hall, kitchen, chapel, reception
chambers, guard rooms and stables; some were duplicated
for the separate use of king and garrison. Internally both
Caernarfon and Conway were divided into wards by a cross-
wall, although with the apparent strength of the surrounding
walls this seems slightly superfluous.

The final development of castle planning was the
concentric lay-out, in many ways the best-known form of
plan in which the main enclosure, the inner ward or bailey,

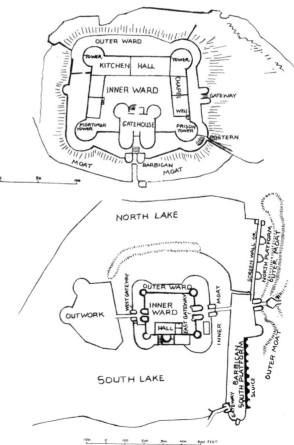

43   Harlech Castle, Merioneth.
1285-90, concentric plan
dominated by the inner gatehouse.

44   Caerphilly Castle,
Glamorgan. 1267-77, concentric
plan with extensive system of moat
and barbican defence.

often rectangular, is surrounded by a further wall lower in elevation than the main towered wall. An excellent example is Beaumaris, another of Edward I's castles, whose outer wall is ringed by mural towers at sixty-foot intervals. As added protection, the southern gatehouse has a barbican to prevent the storming of the inner ward. The outer gates on the north and south sides are built out of line with the inner, so that an enemy piercing the first gates and gaining the lists or outer ward, would be forced to approach the main gate at an angle, thus exposing his flank to attack from archers on the ramparts above. Another impressive example already mentioned is Harlech (p. 63) which because of its position with a cliff edge on its west side, has only one giant inner gatehouse assuming the proportions of a keep of the previous century.

Most castles were surrounded by a moat if there was access to running water, although some were surrounded by a ditch or fosse such as Goodrich in Herefordshire, and Dover, the rocky sides of which would deter most assailants under fire. At Caerphilly, Glamorgan, the castle was built in an immense lake about twelve hundred feet broad. On the east side was an immense platform surrounded by water and acting as a barbican against attack. Unfortunately some of its former grandeur has been destroyed due to the partial drainage of the lake, but Leeds in Kent still retains its full water defence with a disposition on islands similar to Caerphilly.

In many respects the age of the castle ended at the turn of the fifteenth century. The chief reason was the slow decline in its military importance in the later Middle Ages. Warfare was changing from slow drawn-out sieges of strategic castles to struggles between large professional armies in the field. The late Professor Hamilton Thompson has summed up the situation most succinctly: 'A castle like Caerphilly did not put an end to local warfare: it merely warned an enemy off a forbidden track.' There were exceptions, where a castle of major defensive strength was still created, such as Bywell in Northumberland for the powerful Neville family to guard against the ever-present threat of the Scots as late as 1430, and Raglan in Gwent was erected on a grand scale to guard against the continued possibility of local warfare along the Welsh border. In plan it is an irregular enclosure strengthened by polygonal mural towers. Inside, a central range containing the buttery, hall and parlour divides the enclosure into two courts. The castle is dominated by the hexagonal donjon or tower-house standing in its own moat and originally linked to the main complex by a stone bridge. In the south the main threat was the French, and two castles erected during the Hundred Years' War were Queenborough on the Isle of Sheppey from the 1360s which was both perfectly circular and perfectly concentric, and Bodiam, Sussex from about 1385 set in a broad lake fed by the River Rother.

Bodiam for many people is the most romantic of English castles, with its apparent symmetry reflected in the still water of the moat. It is one solid quadrangular unit with the residential apartments behind the high walls; the chapel identifies itself from without by the traceried window. The entrance is through a fine machicolated gatehouse reached across an octagonal outwork, through a now ruined barbican, and across two drawbridges. At each corner of the castle are boldly projecting cylindrical towers, and the centre of the east and west sides is marked by a projecting rectangular tower.

The declining military importance of the castle was marked by increasing domestication to such a degree that in the fifteenth century the fortified manor house began to play a more dominant role, copying features found in castles, but quite obviously not intended to withstand prolonged siege. The tower-house of Tattershall Castle, Lincs. for Ralph Cromwell, Steward to Henry VI, shows the extent to which the castle tradition could still influence the mind of domestic builders; it also marks the first extensive use of brick in England.

Unlike castles, manor houses were essentially for domestic use as the home of a nobleman by birth, or

45   Tattershall Castle, Lincs.
c. 1450, one of the earliest examples
of brick architecture in England;
322,000 were used in its
construction.

inheritance, and his family. The manor might also be the scene of the local court and dispensing of justice, but it was never garrisoned. Before any building was constructed with walls topped by battlements, and so creating a warlike appearance, a 'licence to crenellate' had to be granted by the monarch. This was seen as a sign of trust in his subject by the king. The lord held and administered the surrounding estate in return for an oath of loyalty to the sovereign, and in turn the tenants swore an oath of fealty to their lord.

Most manors were like castles in that they were surrounded by a moat or ditch and a perimeter wall. The lay-out would be dominated by the Great Hall which would be in stone or flint, and from the fifteenth century brick in eastern England. Here the family would pass much of the day in a communal existence alongside the retainers. Entry to the hall would be through a projecting porch leading to a vestibule divided from the body of the hall by a screen. This screen supporting a gallery helped to keep the smell from the kitchen out of the body of the hall. The floor of the hall might be earth, tiles or stone slabs especially if built over a cellar. The centre of the hall would be occupied by an open hearth for the fire, although fireplaces came into fashion from the late fifteenth century. At the upper end would be the high table raised on a dais. Light would come in through windows which were not glazed until the late Middle Ages. The traceried openings would be protected by shutters and lattice slats, glass being rare in all but royal residences. Windows in this state can still be seen at Stokesay Castle hall, Salop from the thirteenth century. Sometimes large bay windows fed additional light to the high table. Roofs were open-timbered, the arch-brace and hammer-beam variety being frequently used. Directly above the central hearth was a louvre in the ridge of the roof through which the smoke escaped.

The walls of the hall were usually rendered in plaster with wooden wainscotting up to about half their height. Towards the close of the thirteenth century tapestry was being made and freely used in England, so that within a hundred years all nobility aspired after hangings of Arras, Paris or London manufacture, a taste retained well into the English Renaissance, when portraits hanging from or set into wall panelling became the means of expressing family status.

The furniture of a medieval hall was scanty – boards on trestles, which could be easily removed, served as tables. At the head of the hall, behind the high table, was a bench seat against the wall and half way along its length, the lord's chair. On special occasions the high table was covered with white linen, and at one side would stand a table with shelves for the display of plate.

As already mentioned, the kitchen was usually at the

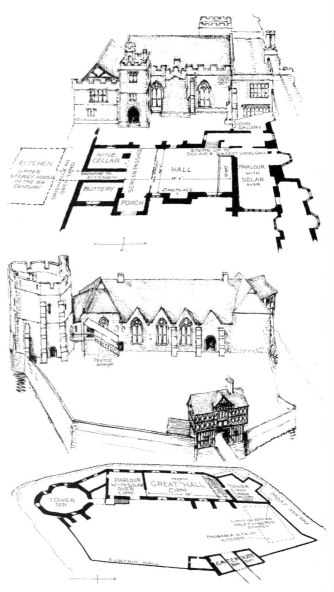

46   *Haddon Hall, Derbyshire.*
c. 1330, one of the most complete
examples of a medieval manor
house with the original central hall
flanked by the buttery and kitchen
on the north, and parlour and solar
at the upper (southern) end. Unlike
Penshurst which had a central
hearth, the hall here seems from the
beginning to have been heated by a
fireplace in the western wall.

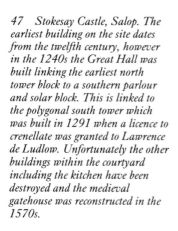

47   *Stokesay Castle, Salop. The*
earliest building on the site dates
from the twelfth century, however
in the 1240s the Great Hall was
built linking the earliest north
tower block to a southern parlour
and solar block. This is linked to
the polygonal south tower which
was built in 1291 when a licence to
crenellate was granted to Lawrence
de Ludlow. Unfortunately the other
buildings within the courtyard
including the kitchen have been
destroyed and the medieval
gatehouse was reconstructed in the
1570s.

lower end of the hall alongside the buttery and pantry,
although sometimes the kitchen was a separate building in
timber and plaster as at Stokesay, and Eltham, London,
both now destroyed. At the upper end of the hall behind the
high table was a door leading into a parlour and possibly a
newel stair to the cellar beneath. This parlour might serve as
an audience chamber or a room for the privacy of the lord.
Alternatively the room or chambers behind the high table
might be used as a sleeping chamber.

A stairway led from the dais to the upper chambers known as the solar (Lat. – *solarium*, a sunny place) which, as the centuries passed, became increasingly a place of comfort and privacy for the family, with glass in the windows and substantial furniture. Adjoining might be a small oratory or chapel, though in some cases this was a separate building as at Cothay Manor, Somerset.

Sanitary conditions were most primitive, and the garderobes were often little more than recesses in the thickness of a wall with outlets discharging at the base of the wall, although where possible they were placed in a projecting turret to discharge into a moat below.

The disposition of other buildings of a medieval manor house varied from site to site. Often the hall was on the far side of a court opposite the gatehouse, as at Stokesay, with ranges including stables enclosing the two remaining sides. Larger manors such as Eltham and Haddon Hall, Derbyshire, developed over several centuries, placed the hall in the centre of the plan with courts on either side. At Eltham the chapel was to the north of the great hall and almost as large. Both were connected on the west to royal apartments, as this was one of the king's most important manors. It has often been said that the medieval manor collected appendages as conditions required. This is why surviving examples have a 'rambling' quality about them, but they provide living witness of continuous occupation down the centuries.

Not all were as complex as Eltham, Haddon or Penshurst. Some, like Ockwells in Berkshire from the 1470s, remain almost as built, with the basic unit of the hall and entrance porch linked at one end to the kitchen with the lower end chamber above; and at the other end is the parlour with the upper end chamber and solar above. The main part of Ockwells is timber-framed with brick laid in herringbone fashion. The windows are large, reflecting the simple Perpendicular style's emphasis on the vertical mullion. A final decorative treat are the carved timber bargeboards on the gables, which provide a pleasing contrast to the battlementing still found at this time on greater domestic buildings.

IX

The Tudor Renaissance 1530-1603

By the time English architecture extensively introduced classical forms or ornament from Italian sources, Bramante, Raphael and Giulio Romano were dead and Michelangelo nearing the end of his long life. The main reasons for England's relative lateness in accepting the artistic Renaissance were the Reformation and her geographical isolation from the Continent. Apart from the tomb of Henry VII in Westminster Abbey and the choir screen in King's College Chapel, Cambridge, little survives of classical detail from Henry VIII's reign. That he employed many foreign craftsmen on royal works is known from surviving records, but the buildings do not survive apart from Hampton Court where terracotta busts of the Caesars by Giovanni da Maiano remain within wreathed niches on the gateway of Clock Court. The greatest of all undertakings, the palace of Nonsuch near Ewell, Surrey, demolished in the 1680s, is known from surviving paintings, engravings and excavation to have been a mixture of French mannerist ornament laid on a basically Gothic plan. It is not however to the crown that we look in the sixteenth century for progressive patronage, but to the nobility, who having profited from the suppression of monastic property, were encouraged to build their homes on an ever-increasing scale.

The source for classical detail at this period was rarely at first hand but rather from foreign treatises on architecture illustrated by engravings of detail, such as columns, capitals, bases and classical statuary used to support horizontal members known as the entablature, architrave and cornice. The most important source in Italian was Alberti's interpretation of the Roman engineer Vitruvius' four books of architecture, which had laid down ornamental proportions followed throughout the Renaissance. Subsequent Italian architectural writers virtually re-interpreted Vitruvius with their own commentary. The first, and rarest architectural treatise published in English was John Shute's 'The First and Chief Groundes of Architecture, 1563. However two works which had a profound influence on Tudor and Jacobean architecture were Sebastiano

Serlio's *Regole generali di architettura* translated into English in 1611, and Andrea Palladio's *Quattro Libri dell' architettura* published in Venice in 1570, although not fully translated into English until 1715.

As well as these and other scholarly works which were of limited circulation due to their being in a foreign language, there developed what are known as 'pattern books', also of foreign origin. These were books of architectural designs and detail which were the work of craftsmen rather than scholars. Accuracy frequently gave way to free invention, especially among the Flemish and German publications such as those of Vredeman de Vries and Wenzel Dietterlin. As far as we know Shute was the first Englishman to visit Italy in 1550, expressly to 'confer with the goings of the skilful masters in architecture, and also to view such ancient monuments thereof as are yet extant'; but it was not until the early seventeenth century and Inigo Jones, that another Englishman followed with the same intention. This, however, is not to suggest that there was little building in England under the Tudors.

Major house plans were of three basic types during the Tudor and also Jacobean periods: E plan, H plan, and quadrangular. The last was popular during the reign of Henry VIII, when the approach to many great houses was still dominated by a battlemented gatehouse as at Hampton Court, Cowdray House in Sussex and Layer Marney Hall,

48   Hampton Court, Great Gateway: c. 1530 (left) as it appears today; (right) as it was from its construction until the mid-eighteenth century, when two storeys were removed.

49   Kirby Hall, Northants.
c. 1570, the first use of Giant
Order pilasters in England. The
range on the left is ruined.

Essex. The third of these shows the increasing use of red brick with dark grey diaper patterning. The dressings of the windows and the parapets are of cream-coloured terracotta. Another brick-and-terracotta building is Sutton Place, Guildford, which originally had a tall entrance gatehouse. In the wing directly opposite is the hall, placed at the centre rather than to one side as was often the case, thus creating symmetry, a characteristic of the classical style to come.

A quadrangular-planned house from the reign of Elizabeth I, showing a much stronger application of classical detail, is the partially ruined Kirby Hall, Northants, begun in 1570 and in stone throughout. Here for the first time in England, giant orders are used for Ionic pilasters, a translation from Italy via France and the influence there of Philibert de l'Orme. The plan consists of a north entrance front and loggia, two long wings on either side of the court for guests, and the south range with a central porch dividing the hall on the right from apartments on the left. The symmetry should be observed, with the line of the mullioned windows of these apartments rising through both floors.

It is on the entrance porch at Kirby that we see the use of triple orders starting with Ionic and rising through two versions of Corinthian to the gable – after the then-current French fashion. On the court facade of the north range we have the Italian practice. Kirby has been attributed to John Thorpe, although it is more likely to have been by his father, who was master mason.

It was during the reign of Elizabeth that classical

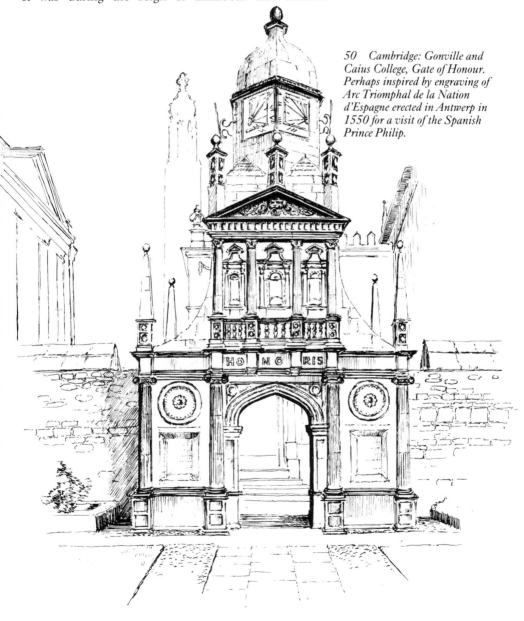

50   Cambridge: Gonville and Caius College, Gate of Honour. Perhaps inspired by engraving of Arc Triomphal de la Nation d'Espagne erected in Antwerp in 1550 for a visit of the Spanish Prince Philip.

*51   Cambridge, Trinity College,
Great Court. The college was
founded by Henry VIII in 1546
and the Fountain exhibiting the
Ionic order was built in 1602.*

ornament became more widely used, not only on domestic
buildings but also, for instance, on gateways such as those of
Gonville and Caius College, Cambridge, of which the Gate
of Honour is the most famous. Above the Doric lower stage,
we have a moulding representing a Corinthian portico in
relief probably derived from an engraving. Built shortly after
the death of Elizabeth, again in Cambridge, the Great Court
of Trinity College is graced with a fountain set beneath an
octagonal canopy supported on Ionic pilasters. Above the
cornice are strap-work screens.

Several of England's most visited stately homes date from
Elizabeth's reign including Longleat, Wilts built for Sir
John Thynne, a courtier under Henry VIII and Edward VI.
Sir Nikolaus Pevsner has called it 'the first house in the truly
English style'. Thynne knew French architecture at first
hand and may have been closely involved in its design, the
master mason was probably Robert Smythson. The plan is
basically rectangular with a central cross-wing creating two
courtyards. The appearance is masterly for the symmetry
and restraint of detail. Each outer façade is divided into
three stages and dressed with classical pilasters on the
projecting bays. In keeping with several other houses by
Smythson, including Wollaton Hall, Notts, and Hardwick

Hall, Derby, the windows extend almost from floor to ceiling in each stage. They are filled with simple mullions and transoms. Beneath the windows of the Ionic and Corinthian stage are classical busts set into circular niches.

The main entrance on the north side is flanked by correctly proportioned Doric columns surmounted by an entablature and broken pediment. Whilst the roof balustrade is markedly horizontal in keeping with the forceful lines of the cornice below, it is broken by gabled adornments displaying French classical idioms, and statues of classical personages. The chimneys are formed from Doric pillars, an idea carried to further extremes at Burghley House, Northants.

For Burghley we know that Lord Burghley collected foreign texts on architecture including those by Delorme whose Château Anet inspired the great central gatehouse. Like Longleat the house is adorned with large windows on each floor, separated by an entablure and cornice. The inner courtyard originally had an open arcade on the ground storey reminiscent of an Italian palace. The gatehouse is of three ordered stages and surmounted by a clock stage which also displays the Burghley family arms and the date of completion, 1585. This is flanked by rampant lions whose tails press against obelisks. The gatehouse is finally topped by a huge pyramid which adds more than an air of

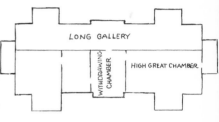

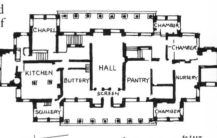

53   Hardwick Hall, Derbyshire, by Robert Smythson, 1590-6, plan.

52   Hardwick Hall. Built for Elizabeth, countess of Shrewsbury, whose cypher is displayed on the parapet. It was designed by Robert Smythson in about 1580 and shows the characteristic of the Elizabethan great house in which there is more window than wall. Classical formality is emphasized by the horizontal cornice divisions.

54   Stonyhurst, Lancs. The house was started in 1592 but remained only half completed until the mid-nineteenth century. The Gatehouse was dressed with four paired orders – the first such use in England. It received cupolas supporting eagles, the emblem of the Shireburn family in 1707. In 1794 the house became the refuge of the Jesuit college from Liège.

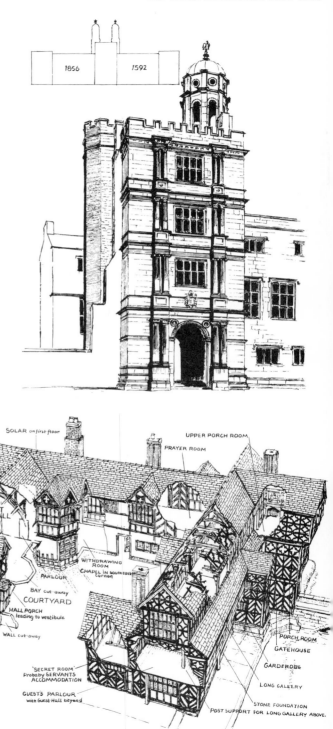

55   Little Moreton Hall, Cheshire.

eccentricity to the skyline already broken by Tuscan-Doric chimneys and miniature gables.

At Wollaton and Hardwick the plan is governed by the hall which in the former is placed in the centre, thus surrounded by domestic apartments. In order to admit light the walls of the hall are carried up above the level of a roof to form a clerestory pierced with windows which look neither Gothic nor classical. The outer façades are of two stages; however the corners are flanked with triple-staged angle towers rising to Flemish-style gables and obelisks.

In 1590 Elizabeth, Countess of Shrewsbury, commissioned Smythson to build a new house for her at Hardwick, in Derbyshire. Here the plan is a wide H with the hall at right angles in the centre, and marks the change from the hall which hitherto normally rose to an open-timbered roof to an enclosed eating-chamber or room on the ground floor. Above the hall runs the Long Gallery which took over in great houses as the centre of social intercourse. At Hardwick it remains, the walls adorned with original

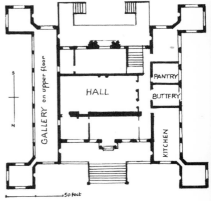

56 Wollaton Hall, Notts. Designed by Robert Smythson and built about 1580-90. The hall rises above the centre with curious clerestory windows, neither Gothic nor Classical. The corner turrets are known as bartizans. The strapwork decoration on the gables of the corner towers should be noticed.

tapestry hangings and portraits; Blickling, in Norfolk, also retains an excellent example of a Long Gallery built in about 1620. The plaster ceiling is decorated with low relief strapwork. In the Great Presence Chamber at Hardwick the plaster frieze on the walls is even more elaborate, depicting Diana and her court hunting. Below, the walls are panelled with geometrical designs and pilaster divisions.

Many houses at this period however showed little sign of a classical renaissance; typical is Montacute, Somerset, where the most noted features are the Flemish gables on the wings. In some cases it is only the stone triple-ordered centrepiece which makes one aware of change, as for instance at Stonyhurst, Lancs., and Cobham Hall, Kent. Whilst brick was now extensively used, there are several notable examples in timber, such as Rufford Hall, Lancs., and Little Moreton Hall, Cheshire. The latter, built for a London merchant William Moreton, is constructed round three sides of a court surrounded by a moat. The timber frame is built on a stone base, and the upper stages are jettied. The hall opposite the gatehouse rises through two storeys, and the walls are 'more glass than wall'. The white plaster infilling between the timbers is divided into various patterns, including quatrefoils creating the characteristic 'magpie' style common in Cheshire and neighbouring counties.

X

The Jacobean style 1603-25

Unlike the political world, artistic taste does not change immediately with the accession of a new monarch. The Jacobean style may therefore be seen as a further development of characteristics which were born during the previous reign. Like the age of the Tudors, the time of James I was not one of church building, with a few exceptions.

Country-house planning gradually discarded the quadrangular plan in favour of the E or H variety. Brick was more than ever used, stone being reserved for ornamental centrepieces except in areas where it was readily available. Roof lines were either marked by a balustrade with repeating open-tracery decoration as found at Bramshill, Hants and Charlton, London, or broken with lines of Flemish gables as found at Blickling.

Hatfield House may be considered as representative of this period. It is an E-plan with the south front of stone joining the two large brick wings. It has an arched loggia on the lower stage displaying Doric pilasters. The gallery above is dressed with Ionic pilasters paired in the centre and increased to a third storey to incorporate the Corinthian order. Behind rises a clock tower and cupola similar to Blickling Hall. The wings were planned to incorporate state apartments for the king on the east, and for the owner, Robert Cecil, Earl of Salisbury, Burghley's second son, on the west. On these wings stone was reserved for the windows which now tended to be smaller than those in Elizabethan mansions, and for quoins set into the corners. A feature almost unique to the Jacobean period are the corner staircase turrets terminating in ogee-curved caps also found at Blickling and Charlton. Rows of brick chimney stacks, some exotically moulded, often graced the roof ridge of a Jacobean house.

The centrepiece of Hatfield south front is fairly formal, but not so that of Charlton, nor Aston Hall, Birmingham which breaks into a riot of classical mannerist ornament – borrowed from German and Flemish sources. Pilasters become tapered stumps adorned with strapwork and topped

57 Charlton House, south-east London, 1607-12. Projecting centrepiece with pilaster adorning first storey derived from book of the orders by Wendel Dietterlin of Nuremberg.

80

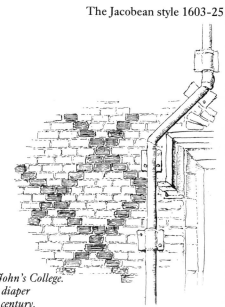

58 *Albury, Surrey. Chimney c. 1600.*

59 *Cambridge, St John's College. Brickwork displaying diaper pattern, late fifteenth century. Drainpipe perhaps contemporary.*

60 *Charlton, Wiltshire. Strapwork ceiling in plaster.*

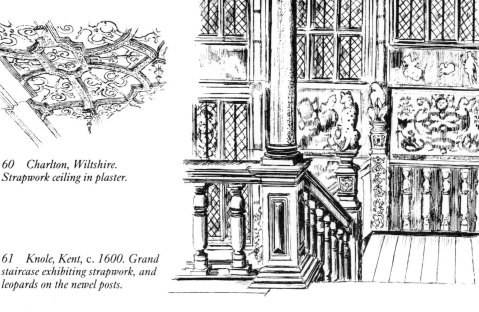

61 *Knole, Kent, c. 1600. Grand staircase exhibiting strapwork, and leopards on the newel posts.*

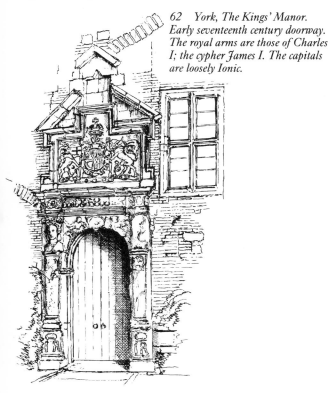

62 York, The Kings' Manor. Early seventeenth century doorway. The royal arms are those of Charles I; the cypher James I. The capitals are loosely Ionic.

Dutch gable

Pedimented gable

Crow-stepped gable.

63 Seventeenth-century gables.

with human heads supporting capitals. A further addition to the centrepiece of Bramshill is a bowed oriel window.

Interiors were now divided into a number of rooms, each with their own purpose and with the emphasis on privacy. The dining hall was used by the family for meals, and the entertainments which had taken place there hitherto now took place in the Long Gallery. The walls were usually panelled with nearly square divisions or occasionally relief strapwork, which is also found on ceilings. An excellent Jacobean Long Gallery survives at Chastleton, Oxon.

Staircases first assume importance during this period. Up until now they had been relegated to towers or the recesses of a house. Now they took a more prominent place sometimes at the dais end of the hall leading up to the Great Chamber. Stairs were in two or three flights with carved strapwork newel posts and balusters. Sometimes, as at Knole, Kent, and Hatfield, the newel posts were surmounted by grotesque animals, or putti. At Hatfield gates survive on the lowest flight to keep dogs from ascending the stairs.

The other major points for decoration of a high quality were fireplaces in dining halls and long galleries. These were normally of stone or alabaster, and the opening was flanked by pillars displaying the orders, or semi-caryatids and terms derived from pattern books. These might support a formal entablature and cornice. Above would be the chimney breast covered with stone moulding or wooden panelling with carvings with a loose classical flavour.

TUSCAN DORIC

GREEK DORIC

IONIC

CORINTHIAN

COMPOSITE

64   *The Classical Orders.*

XI

The age of Inigo Jones 1615-50

Inigo Jones (1573-1652) may be called 'England's first architect' in the sense that he held a professional appointment to design buildings, having first made a prolonged study of classical and Renaissance architecture on the Continent. Jones was born in London, the son of a Smithfield clothworker; we know little of his early life until 1603, when he is named among the Earl of Rutland's retinue visiting Italy as 'Henygo Jones, a picture maker'. This is a reference to his profession at the court of James I where he was employed to design the scenery for court masques. From the surviving designs he seems to have amassed a considerable architectural knowledge before his second trip to Italy in 1613-15, having for a short time prior to this been Surveyor to Henry, Prince of Wales, who died in 1612.

This second Continental journey started in the train of the greatest early-seventeenth-century art connoisseur, the Earl of Arundel, whom Jones escorted as far as Heidelberg. He then made his way south to Italy visiting Venice, Vicenza, Florence and Rome with the intention of studying classical and contemporary architecture. For this he took a copy of Palladio's *Quattro Libri dell' archittetura*, in the margin of which he wrote his own observations as he compared the descriptions with the actual sites. His copy is kept at Worcester College, Oxford. The return journey to England passed through France where he saw some of the Loire châteaux and noted the early Renaissance influence on building in Paris. Jones may therefore be considered the first English architect to visit Italy since John Shute in 1550, and to have had first-hand knowledge of the classical orders and their correct proportion.

Whilst Jones adopted Palladio as his main teacher, he did not slavishly copy his works or the detail of his text. He read the other Renaissance authors who, like Palladio, derived their rules from Vitruvius, but argued rightly that since Vitruvius had lived in about 30 BC he could not have known of the full, and indeed, most magnificent accomplishments of Roman architecture. Where possible Jones met practising

*65   The Queen's House,
Greenwich, 1616-35, by Inigo
Jones. Below – original plan astride
the Woolwich Road.*

SOUTH FRONT

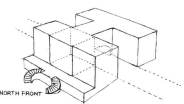

NORTH FRONT

architects, including Palladio's closest pupil, Vincenzo
Scamozzi, with whom he did not get on. Shortly after Jones'
return to England he was appointed Surveyor of Works to
James I and subsequently to his son, Charles I.

Like those of many great personalities in the history of art,
the reputation of Inigo Jones rests on only a few surviving
works. In the case of Jones, whilst many buildings are
attributed to him without documentary evidence, others
remained at the drawing-board stage, such as the projected
rebuilding of Whitehall Palace, or were cut short by the
outbreak of the Civil War in 1642.

Inigo Jones' first commission was granted by the king in
1616 for a hunting villa adjoining the palace of Greenwich
for his queen, Anne of Denmark. Although known today as
the Queen's House it was not completed until 1635 long

*66   The Banqueting House,
1619-22, showing original
appearance with casement windows.
The centre is given prominence by
the use of pillars in contrast to flat
pilasters on either side.*

after her death. Its plan is unusual, two rectangular blocks linked (originally) by one bridge across the former London to Woolwich road. It is built largely of brick and faced with plaster, with stone reserved for window dressings, the dividing plat-band, and the balustrade. It is not modelled on any one Italian source, but on several villas by Palladio and Sangallo the Younger. The immediate impression is one of symmetry, each major front being divided into three with a central projection. The ground floor is given greater impact by the plaster rustication. The north front is raised on a terrace with two curving flights of stairs at its centre, whilst the south front overlooking Greenwich Park is adorned with an Ionic loggia across the central projection at the upper floor.

The Banqueting House, Whitehall, 1619-22, is the first wholly classical building completed in England, built on a restricted site to replace the Jacobean building burnt down in January 1619. Its plan is that of a double cube 110 x 55 x 55 feet with a hall rising through two storeys raised over a basement. Several design elevations by Jones survive; he first intended the façade to be marked in the centre with a pediment. This he abandoned as he adopted Palladio's two-stage façade-type divided by a strongly marked horizontal cornice reminiscent of Palladio's Palazzo Barbarano. As at Greenwich, the centre is projected slightly and further emphasised by pillars instead of pilasters in the side bays. The orders used are Ionic with Composite above, and each end of the building is terminated by paired pilasters – a Venetian mannerist motif for visual effect. Rustication is used for the basement, and the building is constructed throughout in stone.

The interior is a beautifully proportioned single room with a gallery round it supported on consoles at the level of the external cornice, an idea first projected for the 40-foot

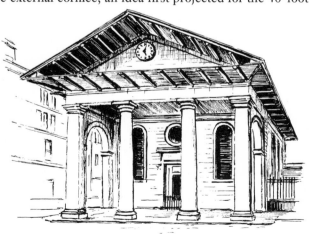

67   St Paul's Church, Covent Garden. It looks rather top-heavy due to the raising of the street level to obliterate the steps, shown in several seventeenth-century engravings.

cube-hall in the Queen's House, Greenwich. The ceiling panels were inset with Rubens' painting of the 'Triumphal Reign of James I' in 1635 or 1636.

Another major royal work started in 1623 was the Queen's Chapel of St James's Palace, built for the Catholic consort of Charles I, the French princess Henrietta Maria. It is a simple plaster-covered rectangular hall, stone being reserved for the quoins at the corners, window dressings and roof pediments. The east front is adorned with a 'Venetian' window – a feature more likely Florentine in origin – and the interior is covered with a coffered barrel ceiling copied directly from antique Roman sources.

Two other major London works by Jones, although not for the Crown, were the Covent Garden Piazza and the restoration of Old St Paul's Cathedral. Covent Garden, started in 1631, was the first serious attempt at classical town planning in Britain, influenced by Jones' visit to Vicenza, Rome, and Paris, where the Place des Vosges (1605) was the most obvious inspiration. The land hitherto was part of the Earl of Bedford's estate inherited from Westminster Abbey at the Dissolution. The piazza was enclosed on the north and east sides by brick terraces raised on arcades as at the Place des Vosges. Ionic pilasters separated the windows, and a classical formality was emphasized by the upper cornice and balustrade.

The west side of the piazza is dominated by St Paul's Church, of plain brick apart from the severe Tuscan-Doric portico, which now looks far too heavy due to the raising of the modern street level to the top step of the base. The sides of the portico are filled with arches derived from the loggia of Palladio's Palazzo Chiericati, Vicenza. Few visitors to Covent Garden realize that this portico does not mark the entrance to the church (which is at the west front), but is purely for the appearance of the piazza. By the 1660s it was the scene of a market, permanent buildings for which were created in the nineteenth century, by which time Jones' arcaded terraces had disappeared.

St Paul's Cathedral was in a severe state of decay when Jones was asked to formulate a plan for its restoration. He proposed enclosing the walls in new stone and imposing classical ornament on the exterior. At the west end he proposed two classical towers (incorporating one from the existing church of St Faith) and a Corinthian portico of eight columns. By the outbreak of the Civil War in 1642 the nave had been encased externally and the windows classicized. The portico was to survive the Great Fire of 1666 and Wren considered incorporating it into the new cathedral.

Jones' work for patrons outside London included advising on the rebuilding of Wilton House, Wilts., although Isaac de Caux was in charge. The south front, started in 1636, looks rather severe apart from the Venetian window in the centre. At each corner are square pedimented towers, a feature to be adopted by the eighteenth-century Palladian movement. The interior is outstanding, especially the Single – and Double – Cube Rooms created after a fire in 1649 by Jones' pupil and nephew by marriage, John Webb. The Double Cube Room incorporates a magnificent collection of framed portraits of the Pembroke family by Van Dyck. The walls are adorned with swags and drops, beneath a highly ornate frieze and cornice. The doorcases have Corinthian pilasters and entablatures supporting broken pediments incorporating the Pembroke arms. The painted ceiling by Edward Pierce is 'coved' or curved from the central oval panel to the wall cornice to create an added dimension to the room.

At the outbreak of the Civil War Jones naturally supported the Royalist cause. He was captured by Parliamentarian forces at the siege of Basing House, Hants., in 1645. It seems that he was pardoned, perhaps because of his age, and was given a pension and accommodation in Old Somerset House where he died in 1652. Buildings attributed to him (but without firm evidence) include Lindsay House, Lincoln's Inn Fields from the 1630s, where

68 *Eltham Lodge, c. 1665.*
Hugh May based the design on that
of the Mauritshuis (top) at the
Hague, by Jacob van Campen,
c. 1630.

giant ordered pilasters rise from a rusticated basement. The windows of the 'piano nobile' are dressed with alternate triangular and semicircular pediments, and the façade is terminated by a boldly projecting cornice and balustrade. Another example is Castle Ashby, Northants, dating from the 1580s, which has a gallery of stone attributed to Jones built across the fourth side of the court in the 1630s. The ground storey has a French flavour, but the upper is more restrained in its classicism.

Jones' closest follower was his nephew John Webb (1611-72) who had become his assistant in about 1628. He worked with Jones at Wilton and on plans for rebuilding Whitehall Palace. Two works by Webb which owe much to Jones include Lamport Hall, Northants, and the King Charles' Block of about 1665 for the proposed rebuilding of Greenwich Palace and later incorporated in the Royal Naval Hospital founded in 1694.

Whilst the age of Charles I witnessed a closer understanding of Italian Renaissance architectural principles, there was still much variation in styles, including the Dutch of Crooms Hill Rectory, Greenwich, and the Dutch House at Kew – both in brick; the Gothic at Oxford in Wadham and Jesus Colleges; and the Baroque (see glossary) in the porch of the church of St Mary the Virgin (1637), perhaps inspired by Bernini's baldacchino in St Peter's, Rome, from about 1625. Country houses tended to be smaller than in the preceding century. Coleshill, Berks, by the gentleman amateur, Sir Roger Pratt started in about 1650 (destroyed by fire in 1952) is typical of the age. It had a rectangular plan with the hall given over to the entrance staircase. Behind was the Great Parlour or salon, a planning disposition to be followed elsewhere during the next 150 years. The exterior was simple with subtle window divisions. A plat-band divided the storeys below a hipped roof, one with sloping ends, and crowned in the centre with a cupola or banqueting house. Another house from the 1650s is Thorpe Hall, Northants, with one of the first projected entrance porticoes in England by a local builder, Peter Mills. The Dutch influence can be clearly seen at Eltham Lodge, London (1663-4) by Hugh May, whose wide travels had included a stay at The Hague: he closely copied the Mauritshuis (1630). Both buildings have pedimented centrepieces on the major façades against hipped roofs which project out beyond the walls to form eaves. Beneath the eaves modillions of wood project to create the effect of teeth. As at Pratt's Coleshill, the chimneys form an integral part of the design of the house, to be seen and not hidden behind a parapet. The windows are of the sash type which, hitherto assumed to have been introduced from Holland in the second half of the seventeenth century, may have been invented in England.

XII

Sir Christopher Wren 1632-1723

The name Wren is almost a household word, even though his documented work is largely confined to London, Oxford and Cambridge. A scientist by profession, he was assisted in achieving architectural greatness by two important facts, the fire of London in 1666 and an unusually long life of 91 years. He was the son of the rector of East Knowle, Wilts., and was educated at Westminster School and Wadham College, Oxford. Such was his brilliance – 'that miracle of youth' Evelyn called him – that he was asked to remain at Oxford as 'demonstrator in Mathematics' until his appointment as Gresham Professor of Astronomy in London in 1659. He returned to Oxford in 1661 as Savilian Professor of Astronomy, and with the granting of a charter by Charles II to the Royal Society in 1662 became its first Secretary.

Although Wren was invited to go to Tangiers in 1662 to advise on the fortification of this Portuguese possession ceded to England as part of the marriage dowry of Catherine of Braganza, an offer he declined, his entry into architecture took place almost by accident. Gilbert Sheldon, Archbishop of Canterbury, granted a bequest to Oxford University for a building suitable for the conferring of degrees, and Wren was called upon, no doubt due to his mathematical knowledge, to design the Sheldonian Theatre in 1663. For this commission he adapted the D-shaped plan of the Theatre of Marcellus in Rome, shown in Serlio's treatise on architecture. Unlike Jones, Pratt and May, Wren was not widely travelled, except that in 1665 he visited Paris and there met Bernini, then working on a design for the East Front of the Louvre; Wren derived his knowledge of past and contemporary Continental architecture largely from engravings.

The Sheldonian Theatre is not Wren's greatest work; however it does show admirably his ingenuity in solving spacial problems. Here in order to retain the effect of a classical amphitheatre open to the sky, he suspended the ceiling panels beneath a system of enormous interlocking roof trusses from wall to wall. The panels were painted to

*69   Wren's versatility as a designer
of churches*

*(left) St Benet, Paul's Wharf. A
simple rectangular design in two-
tone brick with stone quoins at the
corners and a white plat-band
running the length of each façade.
The only decoration is the swags
above each window.*

*(centre) St Magnus the Martyr.
Bears a close similarity to the tower
of St Charles Borromeo, Antwerp.*

*(right) St Dunstan in the East.
Gothic tower added to partially
destroyed medieval church which
was itself rebuilt in 1817.*

70   Wren church plans

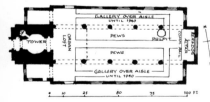

*St Bride, Fleet Street, 1680. Plan
prior to partial destruction in
1940.*

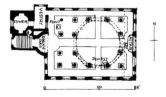

St Stephen, Walbrook, 1672-9.

represent sky, surrounded by canvas awning held open by
ropes simulated by the beading round each panel.

His next two works were at Cambridge: the new chapel
for Pembroke College, and the new chapel and flanking
ranges for Emmanuel College. Both works are strongly
Roman in inspiration, and incorporate Corinthian pilasters
and pediments at both ends. In about 1664 he was asked to
advise on the further restoration of St Paul's, where Jones'
work was incomplete as a result of the Civil War. His short
trip to France in 1665 allowed Wren to see several domical
buildings including Lemercier's churches of Val-de-Grâce
and the Sorbonne, and Le Vau's Collège des Quatre
Nations. These inspired his plan for St Paul's, presented in
August 1666, in which he proposed a great central dome
with a pineapple steeple to replace the medieval crossing
tower.

The Great Fire of 2-6 September allowed Wren perhaps
the greatest opportunity ever presented to a single English
architect to make his impression on one city, although his
plan for a totally new street layout based roughly on a grid
could not be carried out because the freeholders refused to
exchange land for such a radical plan. There was also the
cost of compensation, and the need to house upwards of
150,000 people. Wren, having been appointed a
Commissioner for the rebuilding of London in 1666 and

Surveyor of Royal Works in 1669, relinquished his academic appointments at Oxford, and Gresham College, London, in order to concentrate on architecture.

After the initial rebuilding largely in brick and in conformity with the Parliamentary Act of 1667, work started on the City churches of which 53 were designed by Wren to replace the 109 destroyed in the Fire. Fewer churches were required than before since many parishes were amalgamated. For these a tax on coal unloaded at City wharfs was levied and apportioned to each parish. In these churches, with the problem of extremely confined sites we see Wren at his most inventive. Some were of red Berkshire brick dressed with Portland stone quoins and window surrounds, rather Dutch in flavour, as at St Benet's, Paul's Wharf. Plans ranged from the simple rectangular at St Benet's to the basilican at St Mary-Le-Bow and St Bride. At St Stephen Walbrook, he introduced a dome, the first in England, supported on eight columns within a cruciform plan – a trial run for St Paul's. Whilst Wren left much of the interior decoration and carving to specialist craftsmen, he was closely involved in the design of the towers built of Portland stone and sometimes capped with lead spires. Whilst each one is original, certain features such as the concave faces of the tower of St Vedast, or the peristyle above the belfry stage of Bow, have more than a hint of Borromini and Bramante respectively. The tower of St Magnus the Martyr has a close similarity to that of St

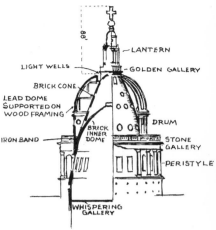

71   St Paul's Cathedral, 1675-1710, showing the influences behind the design of the dome.
(a) Bramante's dome for St Peter's Rome, 1502.
(b) Bramante's Tempietto of S Pietro, Rome, 1502.
(c) Michelangelo's design for dome of St Peter's, Rome, c. 1560.
(d) Jacques Lemercier's dome of Chapel of the Sorbonne, Paris, c. 1640.

Charles Borromeo, Antwerp, from about 1620. Most churches, including several outside the City such as St James's, Piccadilly, were complete for worship by the early 1680s, although towers and steeples were sometimes not added until after 1700.

Wren secured the royal warrant for the rebuilding of St Paul's in 1675. His Great Model, based on a Greek Cross, was heavily indebted to Michelangelo's design for St Peter's, and included a projecting portico against the west front. The warrant design adopted the conventional Latin cross plan of most medieval English cathedrals, however the final version of the dome and west front differs radically. It is likely that Wren planned the detail including the screen walls hiding the nave, choir and transept buttressing as circumstances necessitated. As in his City churches the influence of Baroque masters can be seen, such as Pietro da Cortona in the semicircular transeptal porticos, Bernini and Le Vau in the west front with the paired Corinthian pillars from the Louvre, Borromini in the west towers and Bramante and Michelangelo in the dome. The dome is in fact in three sections: an inner dome to be viewed from the crossing, a brick cone supporting the lantern and raised on the drum, and the exterior lead dome over a timber frame which hides the cone from exterior view. The drum is surrounded by a Corinthian peristyle reminiscent of Bramante's design for St Peter's dome in about 1506. From the exterior Wren has achieved a remarkable effect of height and weightlessness with the lantern seeming to rise from the summit of the outer dome.

St Paul's was opened for worship in 1697 and completed in 1711; however during the period of its construction Wren had also been involved in the creation of many other important projects. At Cambridge in the 1670s he designed the Library of Trinity College, which is of Portland stone and raised on an immense wooden raft sunk into the waterlogged site adjacent to the River Cam. The library itself is at first-floor level above a colonnade to avoid the dampness, an idea perhaps inspired by Sansovino's Library of St Mark in Venice. An inventive note is that the floor level is below that of the external cornice marking the traditional two-stage façade, so allowing adequate bookshelf space below the upper windows. At Christ Church, Oxford, in the 1680s, Wren built Tom Tower in the Tudor Perpendicular style to to fit in with the existing quadrangle; in the City of London he also designed the tower and spire of St Dunstan in the East in the Gothic style.

Wren's major royal work was the state apartments at Hampton Court from 1694 for William III and Mary, in a mixture of orange brick and Portland stone. Each front has a formal classical centrepiece, but the prospect is altogether more homely than Louis XIV's Versailles and exudes a Dutch flavour. Fortunately only part of the original project was carried out as the intention was to demolish the Tudor palace completely. The centre Fountain Court has a grand arcade after the Italian fashion.

At Greenwich, again from 1694, he was responsible for designing the various buildings of the Royal Hospital for retired sailors, a difficult task since he had to incorporate Webb's King Charles Block from the abandoned palace and to provide an open vista from Jones' Queen's House to the Thames, a specific wish of Queen Mary. Again Wren rose to the situation, and with blocks on each side of a central axis closing together, he manages to draw the eye back from the river towards the Queen's House, helped by Doric colonnades against the west and east side of the Queen Mary and King William blocks respectively. Instead of a dominating central domical building as first projected, he mounted Baroque towers over the hall and chapel vestibules.

By the time Greenwich Hospital was finished Wren was a father figure admired by the younger generation of architects such as James Gibbs, yet politically out of favour with the coming to power of the Whigs and the accession of George I. With London's skyline broken by the numerous spires and dominated by St Paul's he could retire to his 'grace and favour' apartment at Hampton Court, knowing that he was a Master whose stature could be measured alongside any of those from seventeenth-century Italy or France.

72   Oxford, Christ Church. Tom Tower, 1681, shows Wren's ability to handle the Gothic style as well as the classical.

73   Cambridge, Trinity College Library, by Wren, c. 1670. Cut open to show floor supported on colonnade below level of outer cornice.

XIII

The eighteenth century: the age of the great house, 1700-30

Although England cannot offer a rival to Versailles, or to Schönbrunn in Vienna, for size in her palaces and country houses, the eighteenth century saw the building of some which can nonetheless be described as overwhelming in appearance and grandeur, and built for a race of 'Augustan' giants. These include Blenheim and Castle Howard by John Vanbrugh and Nicholas Hawksmoor, Seaton Delaval and Kimbolton by Vanbrugh alone, and Chatsworth by William Talman, to mention just a few. In viewing them it is essential to understand that they were built more for effect than convenience and could only be maintained with a large domestic staff to look after the needs of the table as well as the stable.

While no two are the same there is some general similarity in planning. All would have a main rectangular block with the entrance front on the north side where possible, and an equally important garden front on the south so the sun could

74   *Easton Neston, Northants (centrepiece). Hawksmoor's first independent work in the English Baroque tradition.*

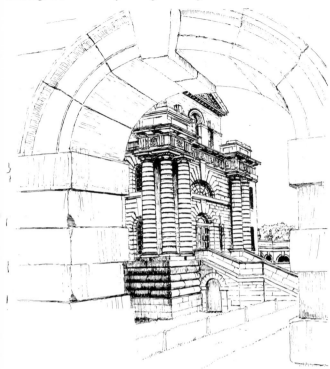

75   *Seaton Delaval, Northumberland. Not as large as Blenheim or Castle Howard but perhaps Vanbrugh at his most dramatic.*

76   *Seaton Delaval. Detail of naval motif in metope of Doric entablature, appropriate for Vanbrugh's patron, Admiral Delaval.*

light the main apartments. Normally this main block was raised on a basement which was rusticated for 'added gravity'. The entrance was reached by straight or curving flights of steps between stone or wrought-iron balustrades. For effect the centre of the façade would be brought forward, and with the abandonment of the traditional two-stage elevation with dividing cornice, the walls would be dressed with giant ordered pilasters as at Hawksmoor's Easton Neston, Northants. The doorway could be further emphasized by columns on either side, or a projecting portico creating the effect of an entrance to a temple, as at Blenheim.

If the house was of considerable importance the main block might be flanked with wings for the kitchen, bakehouse and laundry on one side of the court, and stables and coach-house on the other; Blenheim, started in 1706, is a perfect example. This disposition of buildings helps to emphasize the grandeur of the entrance front, something which greatly appealed to the 'theatrical' nature of playwright-architect John Vanbrugh, and reaching its maximum visual impact at his Seaton Delaval.

The south or garden front would be symmetrical with a pedimented centrepiece or projecting portico. At Castle Howard the main block and flanking wings are dressed with fluted Corinthian pilasters. The centre is emphasized by a pediment. Roofs were normally flat behind balustrades which were decorated at intervals with urns or statuary. Apart from the entablature, pediments and keystones adorning windows, wall decoration was minimal. Therefore the severity of the façades, usually of stone or plaster, was reduced by the careful planting of nearby trees and layout of other garden features such as fountains and terraces.

The entrance led into the hall which was purely for the reception of guests with staircases in chambers on either side leading to the upper floors. At Castle Howard the hall rises to the roof level to be lit by a dome raised on a drum, perhaps an echo by Vanbrugh of Wren's original intention for Greenwich Hospital. Beyond the hall was the salon reserved for banquets and other formal occasions. On either side of the salon was an 'enfilade' of rooms usually lit by the southern light. These included bedrooms, reception rooms and, now indispensable for every 'Augustan' gentleman, a library and a gallery for his collection of antique statues. Gradually the fashion for wooden wall panelling gave way to plaster surfaces divided into bays by pilasters and adorned with a frieze below the coving of the ceiling. The greater houses employed foreign-born artists to paint ceilings and occasionally salon walls, such as the Frenchman Laguerre at Blenheim. Where ceilings were not painted they were decorated with panels or arabesque ornament under the influence of the French rococo style current in England from about 1740.

77   Castle Howard, Yorks. South front of mansion by Vanbrugh and Hawksmoor, c. 1720. The centrepiece is dressed with giant Corinthian ordered pilasters.

1   *Durham Cathedral. Nave from the south aisle, c. 1100, Norman.*

2   Canterbury Cathedral. Choir and
Trinity Chapel begun in 1175, showing
the work of the Frenchman William of
Sens, including sexpartite vaulting.

3   Lincoln Cathedral. Nave from the
south aisle, c. 1230, Early English.

4   Lincoln Cathedral. Angel choir, c. 1270, Early English transitional. The geometrical east window is the largest of its kind. The inner screen of tracery in the clerestory is also noteworthy.

5 York Minster. View from the south east, Early English south transept c. 1225-41; Perpendicular choir c. 1361-1400; central tower c. 1407-20.

6 York Minster. West Front, Decorated, c. 1300-45.

7   Canterbury Cathedral. Nave, c. 1380, Perpendicular, showing strainer arch for central tower, c. 1500.

8   *Lavenham, Suffolk, Parish church, c. 1490, Decorated choir, Perpendicular nave and tower.*

9   *Canterbury Cathedral precincts. Former monastic bakehouse and brewery, now part of the King's School, fourteenth century, built largely in flint with stone reserved for door and window surrounds.*

10   Westminster Abbey. Henry VII Chapel, c. 1503-19, Tudor Perpendicular. The finest example in England of fan-and-pendant vaulting.

11 *Caernarfon Castle, Wales. c. 1290. Rather than a keep, there are enormous mural towers at intervals along the curtain wall.*

12 *Eltham, South London. Great Hall of Palace, c. 1480. Interior before restoration in 1936, showing hammer-beam roof construction.*

13   *Burghley House, Lincs. Elizabethan house showing early use of classical orders, completed 1586.*

14 Holkham Hall, Norfolk. The so-called 'Egyptian Hall', c. 1730, Palladian.

15 St John's College, Cambridge. The Combination Room, 1598-1602.

16   *Senate House, Cambridge, 1722-30, by James Gibbs – a fine example of Palladian simplicity.*

17   *Canterbury. Mid-eighteenth-century brick town house; Ionic ordered doorcase.*

18   Town Hall, Manchester. 1867-77, Alfred Waterhouse. A major civic building of the Gothic Revival.

19 *Bristol. Victorian warehouse on Welsh Back. A mixture of Byzantine elements.*

20 *Manchester. Working-class housing from the mid-nineteenth century, dominated by St Francis's church, Gorton, by E.W. Pugin in the Gothic style, 1864.*

21 *Port Sunlight. Nineteenth-century Garden City, 'Tudor'.*

22 *Canterbury. Semi-detached houses, 1930s 'Tudor'.*

23   Canterbury. Marks and Spencer, c. 1935, 'classical'.

24   Canterbury. University of Kent. Brick-and-concrete collegiate, c. 1970.

25   Newcastle-upon-Tyne. Twenty-storey flats in Westgate Road, mid-1960s.
Three of eighteen blocks providing 1500 homes.

XIV

The Palladian Movement 1715-60

During the eighteenth century architectural taste became bound up with politics. To the rising Whig gentry the creations of Wren, Hawksmoor and Vanbrugh were seen as manifestations of Tory wealth, power and extravagance, but to the man of classical taste they were also a sign of decadence, a deviation from the truth. The Palladian Movement was launched by a series of literary exultations in praise of Inigo Jones and Palladio, and a condemnation of Wren and his school by Lord Shaftesbury in his *Letter on Taste* (1712). In the same year Pope in his *Essay on Criticism* invoked the reader to

> Learn hence for ancient rules a just esteem;
> To copy Nature is to copy them . . . .

In 1715 two further publications were to have a profound effect on the movement and the future of English

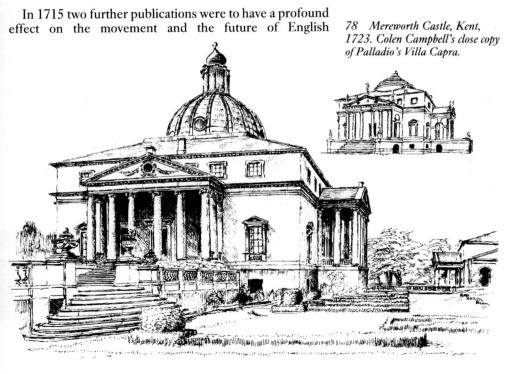

78   Mereworth Castle, Kent, 1723. Colen Campbell's close copy of Palladio's Villa Capra.

architectural taste, the first English translation of Palladio's *Quattro Libri dell' architettura*, and Colen Campbell's *Vitruvius Britannicus*. Campbell's work finally ran to three volumes and was virtually a survey in engravings of most major English classical buildings from Jones' Queen's House started in 1616 up to 1725, the year of the publication of the third volume. Campbell, a Scotsman, arrived in London shortly before 1715 at a time when, in the eyes of many, to be a Scotsman was to be a Jacobite. As a pledge of loyalty he dedicated the first volume to George I.

Campbell argued that Jones was the only English architect to interpret Palladio correctly, and only by going back to Palladio could we understand the 'Antique Simplicity' of Vitruvius. His first volume quickly became the creed of the Whig arbiters of taste, foremost among them Richard Boyle, third Earl of Burlington (1695-1753). Burlington employed Campbell to classicize the family home in Piccadilly, although his best known works which show his allegiance to Palladio and Jones are Mereworth Castle, Kent, and Houghton Hall, Norfolk, both started before 1723.

Mereworth is almost a translation to English soil of Palladio's Villa Capra near Vicenza. The plan is a square with a circular hall in the centre beneath the central dome. Each façade has a hexastyle (six-columned) portico, but unlike the prototype, Campbell's work has flights of steps only on two sides. The dome of Mereworth is however closer to Palladio's intention for the Villa Capra than to the building itself, where Scamozzi had finished the work with a

79   Prior Park, Bath. The Palladian bridge by John Wood the Younger, one of four bridges inspired by an unexecuted design by Palladio.

80   Chiswick House, 1725. Lord
Burlington's villa deriving more
from Scamozzi's Villa Pisani than
from Palladio's Villa Capra.

81   Chiswick House. Salon with
apsidal coffering perhaps derived
from Temple of Venus in Rome
(above).

lower tiled dome. Campbell avoided the use of chimneys by taking the smoke up through flues in the dome to escape beneath the cowl of the lantern. The porticoes used here and on other Palladian buildings were derived from the mistaken notion in Vitruvius' writings that all antique houses had them.

Houghton Hall for the Whig Prime Minister Walpole shows Campbell's derivation from Jones' Wilton House in the corner towers, and the stone hall derived from that in the Queen's House, Greenwich, using the same proportions and incorporating a projected gallery. The lavish plaster decoration on the walls and ceiling is by the Italian, Attari. Unfortunately Campbell's earliest work, Wanstead House, Essex, started about 1712, has been destroyed but its main elevation with hexastyle portico was closely copied by John Wood at Prior Park, Bath, and Henry Flitcroft at Wentworth Woodhouse, Yorks.

The exact contribution of Lord Burlington to the movement apart from patronage is hard to define. He visited Italy twice and knew Vicenza and Rome intimately, subsequently publishing a volume of Palladio's drawings.

82   York, The Mansion House, c. 1730. A civic building in the Palladian style, for some time attributed to Lord Burlington who designed the nearby Assembly Rooms.

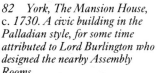

Whilst not giving his name to any specific work – due no doubt to his aristocratic position – he is considered to be the scholarly mind behind the detail of Holkham Hall, just two miles from Houghton, although the general conception was that of William Kent. The plan consists of a central block with linked wings at each corner. At the wish of the owner, Thomas Coke, it was built of local yellowish brick to resemble the colour of that found in Rome's antique remains. Both the north and south fronts feature Venetian windows. The masterpiece of the interior is the so-called Egyptian Hall, flanked by marble Corinthian columns and leading through an apse to the salon behind. The plan of the hall was derived from Palladio's interpretation of Vitruvius' description of an 'ancient basilica' which he could only assume must be Egyptian. The ceiling and apse are coffered and the frieze is derived from the Temple of Fortuna Virilis, in Rome. Burlington was also the designer of the York Assembly Room which is another 'Egyptian' Hall.

In Burlington's villa at Chiswick (1723), we have another interpretation of the Venetian villas of Palladio. It is only loosely based on the Villa Capra, featuring only one Corinthian hexastyle portico. The octagonal drum and dome are in fact copied from Scamozzi's Villa Pisani. Unlike Campbell at Mereworth, Burlington did not abandon chimneys but cleverly disguised them as obelisks. The Villa, intended as a suburban retreat for Burlington and his circle of classical *cognoscenti*, has a variety of room shapes including rectangular, square, round and octagonal. The gallery on the garden side introduces coffered apses at each end, a favourite Palladian feature intended to create the feeling of additional space. The interior decoration is by Kent who was also responsible for the Horse Guards' Building in Whitehall – a smaller interpretation of Holkham in Portland stone.

Other major Palladian architects include Giacomo Leoni (*c.* 1686-1746), a Venetian by birth who, as already mentioned (p. 98), translated Palladio's writings into English, but who also designed several impressive mansions including Lyme Hall, Cheshire, and Clandon Park, Surrey. Sir James Thornhill, better known as a painter, designed Moor Park, Herts., with a huge, four-columned portico, whilst Roger Morris confined his work to medium-sized houses such as White Lodge, Richmond Park, and Marble Hill House at nearby Twickenham, both with pedimented centrepieces incorporating four Doric pilasters. Palladian principles also profoundly affected eighteenth-century town planning, especially in London and Bath, as we shall see (pp. 111-3).

XV

The landscaped garden

It was during the eighteenth century that the English concept of the garden plan moved radically away from the formality of the Continental examples, based on a geometrical arrangement of avenues, hedges and bushes. Under the influence of the 'Grand Tour', indispensable for educated gentlemen, there came the urge to re-create their own version of the Italian landscape on the English country estate. The conviction that this was the 'true' landscape of classical civilization was reinforced by the paintings of Claude and his imitators, avidly collected by the English gentleman.

In order to create such a landscape considerable physical labour was involved in creating mounds and small hills by moving barrow-loads of earth. Sometimes rivers were dammed to form lakes or to create waterfalls or cascades at various levels. Where possible the boundary of the estate was disguised by a ditch or ha-ha with the brick wall hidden out of view from the house. Another man-made 'natural' feature was a grotto sometimes dedicated to Neptune such as that at Stourhead, Wilts., which includes a reclining statue in its depths.

Architecture played a considerable part in creating the illusion of a classical landscape, and indeed, a hint of the medieval, with Gothic follies following in increasing number after Horace Walpole's 'Strawberry Hill'. Often gateways formed an imposing entrance to an estate or park.

83   Sham Castle, near Prior Park, Bath, c. 1760.

This could be in the form of a pedimented classical arch as at Stowe, Bucks., or with side screens and lodges as at Easton Neston. Within the confines of a park or landscaped garden buildings would be disposed at the owner's wish, to create his idea of 'natural perfection'. Whilst specialist landscapists such as Lancelot 'Capability' Brown, William Kent, and Humphry Repton planned the disposition of nature which could never, unfortunately, mature during the patron's lifetime, architects designed the buildings. Today the best remaining estates (garden or park can hardly be used in the conventional sense) are Stourhead, Stowe, Gibside near Newcastle, and Castle Howard, Yorks.

At Stourhead buildings are arranged around or near the lake created by the London banker, Henry Hoare. The visitor approaches the lake past a Gothic cross which originally stood in the centre of Bristol. The most prominent building then comes into view, a quarter-size reproduction of the Roman Pantheon created for Stourhead by Flitcroft. Nearby is a Gothic cottage, a grotto, a Temple of Diana, and away on the horizon, a Gothic folly known as Alfred's Tower.

The plan of Stourhead has the 'architectural ornament' set on slopes to the lake at the lowest level of the estate; however sometimes lakes were planned to fall to a lower level through the series of cascades or waterfalls almost indispensable in a Claude painting. At Chatsworth a tributary of the Derwent cascades over 300 yards, whilst at Prior Park, Bath, a so-called Palladian Bridge crosses an artificial lake above a miniature waterfall (see figure 79). This bridge is virtually a copy of one at Wilton by Roger Morris of 1736 based on unexecuted designs by Palladio. There is a similar bridge, too, at Stowe, Bucks.

Sometimes summer houses or gazeboes were arranged in

84 Stourhead, Wilts. Miniature Pantheon by Henry Flitcroft with original above. On the right is the 'Gothick Cottage'.

85 Bridge at Wallington, Northumberland, c. 1760 by James Paine, a later Palladian architect.

wooded bowers where *al fresco* festivities could take place reminiscent of those in the French rococo paintings of Watteau, Lancret and Boucher. A further hint of the exotic was introduced in the mid-eighteenth century with the cult of chinoiserie. William Chambers designed a pagoda for Kew as part of the various architectural ornaments of the royal garden which also included a Moorish Alhambra.

Since a gentleman's estate was to emphasize visually the claim of a family to generations of ownership it was often felt that even in death one should be bound to one's 'earthly kingdom'. Hitherto a family vault in the neighbouring church or chapel attached to the house was enough. With the eighteenth century came the rise of the mausoleum, a burial monument taking its name from the tomb of the Emperor Mausolus at Halicarnassus. At Castle Howard an enormous Doric-ordered mausoleum over 60 ft high stands isolated on a hilltop over a mile from the house. Most were smaller with a burial vault below ground level. At Cobham, Kent, there is perhaps the most apt design of all for a building commemorating family dynasties, a pyramid for the Darnleys.

86 Imitation Chinese Bridge, Herne Hill, near Faversham, Kent, c. 1900.

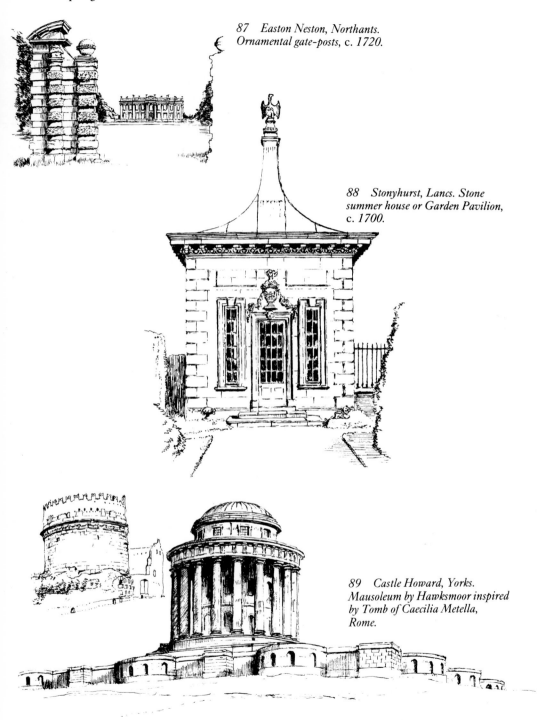

87 Easton Neston, Northants.
Ornamental gate-posts, c. 1720.

88 Stonyhurst, Lancs. Stone
summer house or Garden Pavilion,
c. 1700.

89 Castle Howard, Yorks.
Mausoleum by Hawksmoor inspired
by Tomb of Caecilia Metella,
Rome.

XVI

University buildings in Oxford and Cambridge up to 1800

Until the 1830s Oxford and Cambridge were the only English universities although Scotland had four by the sixteenth century. Both Oxford and Cambridge existed by the early thirteenth century, the former traditionally having been founded for English students barred by political troubles from studying at Paris. Until the fifteenth century most students were attached to private halls but lived in lodgings, often at the mercy of landlords who charged

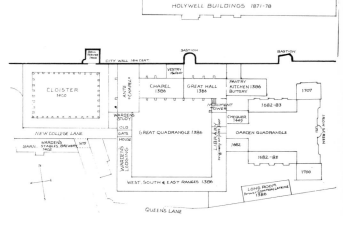

90   New College, Oxford, founded by William of Wykeham, Bishop of Winchester in 1379. Main quadrangle showing chapel and dining hall on left. The range opposite is shown as it was when completed in about 1400, and with additional storey of c. 1684. Sash windows from about 1720.

exorbitant rents. With increasingly bad relations between town and gown, including riots, colleges were founded in which students, at first only graduates, would live and study under the discipline of a principal, often a Master at Cambridge, or Warden at Oxford. The oldest college at Oxford is University College (1249), and at Cambridge Peterhouse (founded 1280).

Until the sixteenth century the buildings were in the Gothic style and normally conforming to a simple

91   Christ Church, Oxford. Peckwater quadrangle by amateur architect Dean Aldrich.

92   Oxford, The Radcliffe Camera, c. 1737-48, finished by James Gibbs although the original idea for a circular building was by Hawksmoor (shown on right). The upper two sketches show Sta Maria della Salute, Venice (left), and the Mausoleum of Theodoric, Ravenna (top right), both influences on Gibbs.
The small sketch on the far right shows Hawksmoor's original model.

quadrangular plan with entry through a crenellated gatehouse. New College, Oxford (founded 1379), retains its main fourteenth-century quadrangle unaltered apart from the addition of an upper storey to each range in the seventeenth century. One side is occupied by the hall and chapel, a plan closely followed at nearby Magdalen (founded 1458). New College also has a small cloister with a bell tower to the side, virtually reproducing the plan of the sister foundation of Winchester College. At Merton College, which has the oldest quadrangle in Oxford (before 1300), the chapel is almost of cathedral proportion although only the choir and transepts were completed. The quadrangle also incorporates what was the first college library, with a few remaining chained books, and a muniment room distinguished by its stone roof to protect college documents, including charters, from fire.

93   Oxford, All Souls College. East side of the Codrington Quadrangle by Hawksmoor in the Gothic.

The Renaissance had only a gradual effect on university architecture until well into the seventeenth century, when Emmanuel and Trinity colleges in Cambridge received additions by Wren (see page 93). Wadham College, Oxford, founded in 1610, retained the traditional medieval plan with a quadrangle entered through a battlemented gatehouse. The eighteenth century saw considerable classical building especially at Oxford although only one college, Worcester at Oxford was founded during this period, in 1714. At King's, Cambridge, a gradual rebuilding on the south side of the chapel was proposed, but only the beautifully proportioned Fellows Building by Gibbs was completed; he also designed the Palladian Senate House nearby. There was a substantial rebuilding of Clare College but this marks the limits of classical building until the early 1800s with the building of Downing College in the Grecian style and the severity of Neo-Classicism.

Oxford saw the total rebuilding of Queen's College from 1709 when Nicholas Hawksmoor was consulted on the plan to rebuild the front quadrangle based on that of a Parisian 'hôtel' or town-house with a screen forming the High Street frontage. The north side of the quadrangle has the hall and chapel divided by a Doric centrepiece inspired by Hawksmoor's work under Wren at Chelsea Hospital. The library beyond was loosely influenced by that of Trinity, Cambridge. Worcester College was built with arcaded blocks round three sides of a quadrangle, whilst a free-standing arcaded block known as the New Building was created in the deer park of Magdalen College.

Dean Aldrich of Christ Church was also an amateur architect of Palladian sympathy. He designed Peckwater Quadrangle and the new library in his own college, as well as the town church of All Saints in the High Street.

The grandest classical building of all at Oxford is the Radcliffe Camera (1737-48), first conceived as a large circular building on a square rusticated base by Hawksmoor with echoes of his Castle Howard mausoleum, but refined and perfected by James Gibbs. Immediately to the east of the Camera, Hawksmoor was building the Codrington Quadrangle at All Souls (1716-35) in the Gothic style.

XVII

The eighteenth-century town

94   Nantwich, Cheshire, Welsh Row. Even though Nantwich was largely destroyed by fire in 1583, it was rebuilt in wood as the remaining half-timbered house shows. Towards the end of the seventeenth century many of the timber buildings were replaced by substantial houses in brick, displaying considerable elegance, especially in the doorcases and pediments. Those shown here date from shortly after 1700.

Before the eighteenth century few towns were more than what we would call large villages today, although the number of communities in England calling themselves towns was perhaps as high as 800. Largest by far was London with a population of about 570,000 in 1700, followed by Norwich and Bristol with 30,000 and 20,000 inhabitants respectively. Liverpool had only about 5,000 people but by 1811 it had grown to over 94,000 and had become the second major port. There is not room here to discuss the reasons for the rapid growth of population but simply to describe the changing architectural environment of an age which saw towns such as Bath break from their medieval confines.

Until well into the seventeenth century the average

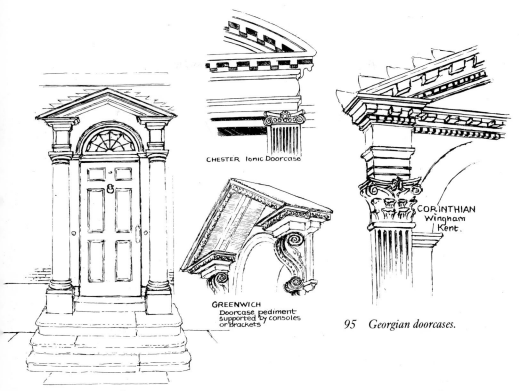

CHESTER Ionic Doorcase

CORINTHIAN
Wingham
Kent.

GREENWICH
Doorcase pediment
supported by consoles
or brackets

95 Georgian doorcases.

GREENWICH Tuscan Doric Doorcase.

provincial town was a disorganized layout of lanes and alleys along either side of one or two main streets. Many were to remain rural in character with gardens or allotments occupying more than half the town area, as can be seen by glancing at any large-scale plan of Canterbury or Leicester from the next century. The only substantial buildings would be the parish church, bridge, guild or town hall, grammar school and almshouse. Outside the stone belt of the Midlands and northern counties many houses were still timber-framed with thatched roofs and small casement windows. The risk of fire was ever-present and outside London there were major conflagrations at Warwick in 1694 and Shrewsbury in 1774. Fire, as well as the lack of good building timber, was one of the reasons for the rapid conversion to brick from the reign of Charles II onwards.

London led the way in seventeenth-century urban development with the layout of western suburbs including Covent Garden, Lincoln's Inn Fields, and St James's Square, virtually linking the City with Westminster. Brick was used throughout except for doorcases, and the houses or blocks were of three or more storeys above a basement.

Until a Building Act of 1707 roofs projected out over wooden eaves-cornices but thereafter were half hidden by a parapet wall. Two years later another Act forbad exposed woodwork in window openings nearly flush with the brick face. Instead the frames were to be set back four inches, so giving a greater sense of solidity to the walls. Both measures were designed to lessen the chance of fire. Wood was still used for doorcases although Portland stone was increasingly used on grand terrace projects. Stucco, popularized by John Nash in the early nineteenth century, frequently covered the basement and ground storey of principal façades.

Brick was often of two tones, 'stocks' of two colours – grey and red for walling in general – and usually laid in the so-called Flemish bond. A more expensive type of brick was the 'cutting brick', crimson in tone and capable of accurate cutting. It was used for the dressing of windows and recesses, and for cornering where stone quoins were not used. An Act of 1739 laid down a standard measure for bricks made within fifteen miles of London.

Roofs over much of England were of tile, or stone shingles, until the late eighteenth century when Welsh slate was exported from the Penrhyn quarries; this was one of the key factors in the disappearance of rustic charm and colour.

The interior disposition of rooms of a terrace house obviously varied according to the number of floors. Since terraces were devised to accommodate the maximum number of homes on a limited site each property was deep and narrow. All houses except the poorest had basements but often of a shallow excavation since the roadway was partly made up. The rear led directly into a court and sometimes then up several steps to a yard or garden.

The ground storey, entered from the front door, typically contained a dining room, parlour and library with a small kitchen to the rear. Above on the first storey were the bedrooms, though in grander houses, sitting rooms may have occupied this floor as well. The second floor was given over to bedrooms or to servants' quarters if there was not room enough within the roof. The master at designing house interiors which contrived to create the effect of maximum space in the minimum area was Robert Adam, who often introduced the oval as a favourite planning element. Unfortunately most of his smaller town interiors have been destroyed.

Until the late eighteenth century interiors were panelled in painted and gilded wood often of Baltic fir, or mahogany from the West Indies; however with Adam came a wider use of plastered walls with shallow relief ornament.

The Georgian period is renowned for the development of the spa town such as Bath and Tunbridge Wells, and also the seaside resort such as Margate, Brighton and

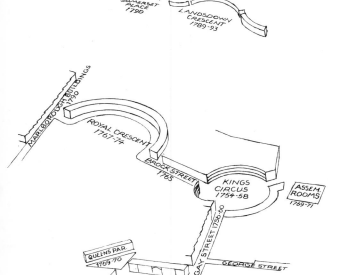

96   *Major features of the Georgian planning of Bath.*

Weymouth. The inland spas were laid out with a formality hitherto reserved for the Continent. At Bath John Wood the Elder, and his son, created a number of thoroughfares linking squares, a crescent and circus on what was hitherto open hillside. This formality was continued after their deaths by John Eveleigh and Thomas Baldwin. Adam created one masterpiece at Bath, the Pulteney Bridge over the Avon, so allowing the development of Batheaston.

The Woods' work is essentially Palladian with the intention of creating a 'Roman' spa. The Circus has been likened to the façade of the Colosseum in reverse with three

97   *Bath: Queen Square, north side. John Wood the Elder, 1728.*

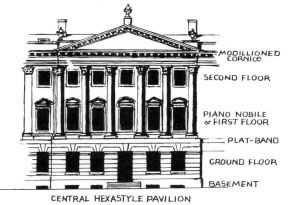

98 *Buxton, Derbyshire. The Crescent, John Carr of York, 1779-81.*

stages dressed with the Doric, Ionic, and Corinthian order. The Royal Crescent relies for much of its effect on the sloping parkland in front to set off the gently curving façade dressed with giant ordered Ionic pillars rising through two storeys. At Queen's Square we have the perfection of the Palladian terrace with a pedimented centrepiece and corner pavilions; Wood the Elder had previously worked in London on the building of Cavendish and Grosvenor Squares. Other spa towns such as Buxton and Cheltenham adopted the features of Bath although the most imposing formal Georgian layout is Edinburgh New Town, partly by Adam. Sometimes towns introduced these elements in isolation as in the Crescent at Ramsgate, or Paragon (in brick) at Blackheath.

The Georgian period proved that imposing domestic architecture need not necessarily be in stone as was the case in Bath and Buxton. With the growth of the mercantile class centred in towns with an export outlet through a port or with good lines of communication, carefully planned streets were laid out with brick terraces of three or more storeys. Liverpool still retains many from the late Georgian period with frontages retaining their pilastered porticoes and fanlights above the doors. Often the date of construction is stamped on to the head of drainpipes. In order to prevent passers-by or visitors from falling into the basement wrought iron railings protected the frontage and steps to the front doors. Iron balconies were also frequently introduced to first floor windows. At Bath, Liverpool and Edinburgh

99   Blackheath, The Paragon,
c. 1806. Seven brick houses linked
by Doric colonnaded wings in the
plan of a shallow crescent.

100   Doorway, Adam period,
c. 1775. St James's Square,
London. Worthy of note is the
delicate lead framed fanlight.

fine iron lampholders still frequently flank the entrances.

Unfortunately few genuine shopfronts remain from before the beginning of the nineteenth century, although we can still often identify the nature of the trade carried on in a particular quarter of a town by surviving street names such as Fish Street, Drapers' Lane, Butchers' Row or the Shambles. By about 1700 shop fronts had acquired glass in the main streets of London and the larger provincial towns, although away from the fashionable areas most shops had wooden shutters which were let down to form a counter for the sale of wares. As late as the mid-nineteenth century Butchers' Row, Coventry had not a single glass-fronted shop. York has a number of late Georgian glazed, bowed shopfronts with rectangular panes of glass set into a wooden frame. The doorways have iron fanlights with glazing bars; No 37 Stonegate has the trader's coat of arms carved in wood over the door. London has two impressive shopfronts, No 56 Artillery Lane, Spitalfields, c. 1757, with windows and doors flanked by Doric pillars supporting a wooden entablature, and No 34 Haymarket (formerly Fribourg and Treyer).

Among public buildings of prominence would be the town hall, mansion house, or guildhall where the mayor and corporation would meet. Some were set in the centre of a town at the junction of main streets as at Abingdon, Oxon.

101   Edinburgh, Moray Place,
c. 1820, Gillespie Graham. One of
the most impressive parts of the
New Town which rivals Bath in
the quality and surviving number
of Georgian buildings.

(1677), where Christopher Kempster created a stone building raised on an arcade and dressed with Corinthian giant pilasters. At nearby High Wycombe the Guildhall of about 1760, on a colonnade, is restrained in the Palladian fashion. Both examples are surmounted by a cupola. The Palladian influence is strong in the Mansion House, York, from about 1730, with its rusticated ground storey and pedimented centrepiece on four Ionic pilasters (see figure 82). Liverpool has one of the finest town halls in England, designed by John Wood the Elder in 1749. It was intended that the ground storey should act as an exchange for the merchants to transact their business, whilst municipal functions would take place on the floor above. The impressive dome on a high 'Baroque' drum is by James Wyatt, and the Corinthian portico by John Foster.

Sometimes a corporation ran a charity school for the education of poor children. An excellent surviving example in the Wren manner is the Bluecoat School, Liverpool, from about 1717. Almshouses also survive in considerable number, and range from the simple and quaint to the impressive, like Morden College, Blackheath, 1695, attributed without foundation to Wren and built in the 'Dutch' style on a quadrangular plan. It retains its window shutters. Other public buildings, often of architectural note, include assembly rooms – there are good examples at Bath and York.

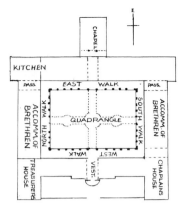

102 Morden College, Blackheath, 1695-1702. Founded by Sir John Morden for 'Decayed Merchants in the Turkey Trade'. It is typical of the domestic brick architecture of the age of William and Mary and is built in red brick with stone quoins at the corners and a prominent plat-band dividing the stages. The accommodation of the brethren is ranged round a quadrangle, and the external appearance of the almshouse remains virtually unaltered.

XVIII

The battle of styles 1700-1900

The Gothic Revival

Whilst the Renaissance marked the rebirth of the classical style it did not mean a complete break with the Gothic in England. As we have seen, the Gothic style lingered throughout the seventeenth century, used especially at the two universities. In some respects therefore, it is misleading to talk of a Gothic revival in the early eighteenth century, although there was a growing movement to cultivate the 'medieval'. Vanbrugh's 'Bastille' at Greenwich from 1717 is not truly Gothic, yet it shows the tendency, prevalent among many gentry of the period, to play with Gothic as if it were a 'toy', as Horace Walpole did at his Strawberry Hill.

A careful comparison between many eighteenth-century Gothic buildings and medieval examples will show the differences immediately: the revived Gothic style is characterized by pointed windows without tracery, a passion

103   Vanbrugh Castle, Greenwich, 1717. It looks at its most dramatic when silhouetted against the moonlit sky over East Greenwich.

105   Frampton Court, Glos. The Gothic Garden House, c. 1760.

for ogee arches, pinnacles without buttressing and sometimes placed over windows, false machicolation, towers of a disproportionate height, and interiors decorated from floor to ceiling with arched and circular Gothic moulding, carved, painted or plastered. Walpole's Strawberry Hill is the best example, as one can trace the owner's taste over a period of forty years from 1749 when he purchased a small cottage in Twickenham. He sought the advice of a committee which included William Robinson, Thomas Pitt and John Chute, who were to design rooms and furnishings on the model of suitable buildings such as Westminster Abbey and Canterbury Cathedral. The house became a 'must' for distinguished visitors to London, who would come to 'breakfast with Mr Walpole' and view his collection of paintings and 'curiosities' amid his pie-crust Gothic interior.

The interest in the Gothic was fired by a number of novels which evoked a lost medieval world, not least Walpole's *Castle of Otranto* which purported to be the translation of a long-lost manuscript. The passion for the Gothic was to be parodied in Jane Austen's *Northanger Abbey*, but not before James Wyatt had built the extravagant Fonthill Abbey for the millionaire eccentric William Beckford. Built largely in the Decorated style, it was dominated by a 280-foot tower loosely modelled on the octagon at Ely. Other patrons were less extravagant, sometimes commissioning a Gothic summerhouse or folly for their estates.

Although the eighteenth century saw some impressive classical churches, there were a number in the Gothic. The

104   Strawberry Hill, Gothic Revival window, c. 1750.

rebuilding of Shobdon, Hereford, is attributed to William Kent. Its interior might be described as an ecclesiastical ballroom, so delicate is the decoration. Galby Church, Leics., has Gothic features including a pinnacled tower and traceried windows amid restrained classical horizontality. Few tourists realise that the western towers of Westminster Abbey are by Hawksmoor and date from about 1730.

Towards the end of the century the Gothic began to take a more serious and scholarly character with a growing interest in archaeology. Several cathedrals including Salisbury underwent extensive (some would say ruthless) restoration at the hand of James Wyatt. In the nineteenth century the movement became a crusade likened by A.W.N. Pugin to the cause of 'Christian truth' over classical paganism. The truth was proclaimed in a number of books by Pugin and others, including Thomas Rickman who first used the terms Early English, Decorated and Perpendicular, to define the various phases of Gothic in an essay published in 1817. Rickman's most important work was the New Court of St John's College, Cambridge in the Tudor style. It was at Cambridge that the Gothic was fervently promoted with the foundation of the Camden Society in 1841, and its monthly journal *The Ecclesiologist*; many colleges subsequently undertook extensions in the Gothic style.

A.W.N. Pugin (1812-52), a convert to Catholicism, will forever be associated with the rebuilding of the Houses of Parliament from 1836, yet it was a joint undertaking with Sir Charles Barry; Catholics were officially barred from entering the design competition. The brief was for a

106   Cambridge, St John's College. Thomas Rickman's Gothic bridge, 1827-31, linking the seventeenth-century court to the nineteenth-century extension on the west bank of the Cam.

107   Westminster, Houses of Parliament. Barry and Pugin's successful combination of late Gothic ornament. The Victoria Tower is reminiscent of a 'Perpendicular' cathedral crossing tower, and inspired the French artist Monet to paint it against a misty sunset.

building in the Perpendicular style to harmonize with the surviving Westminster Hall and nearby Henry VII Chapel. The result was a success, the symmetry of the river frontage set off by the differing heights of the various towers. Pugin also designed many other successful buildings including Scarisbrick Hall, Lancs., 1837, and a number of churches including St Giles's, Cheadle, Staffs., in the Decorated style, and St Mary's, Derby, in the Perpendicular.

The Gothic revival spread rapidly to the Continent and especially Germany, where Goethe had written in praise of Strasbourg Cathedral. In time the movement led to the completion of a number of medieval cathedrals including Cologne which was inspired by the then restoration work at York. It was at Hamburg in 1846 that Sir Gilbert Scott (1811-78) won his first major commission, for the church of St Nicholas, in the 'middle-pointed' but crowned with a typically German open-tracery spire. Scott's architectural output was immense, including churches, schools, colleges, houses, memorials and most memorable of all, the Midland Hotel at St Pancras Station. It is adorned with tiers of arcading set into a red-brick façade. The immensity of the main entrance has the flavour of North German brick Gothic. The magic of this building is completed by the numerous chimneys and pinnacles and a clock tower, all best seen at dusk. His chapel for Exeter College, Oxford (1857-9) was inspired by the Sainte-Chapelle, Paris.

During the age of Victoria the Gothic style could be adapted for any purpose, whether it be the railway tunnel at

Bramhope, or the Law Courts in the Strand by G.E. Street, and French in feeling. St Edmund's School, Canterbury, by P.G. Hardwick, is a perfect example of 'public school architecture'; the Prudential Assurance Building in Holborn is by Alfred Waterhouse – here again there is a feeling of north German massiveness in the entrance tower. Waterhouse was also responsible for the magnificent Natural History Museum at South Kensington (1873-9), inspired by the German Romanesque and close in feeling to the contemporary Hanover railway station. Using horizontal bands of yellow and purple terracotta, he followed the fashion of polychromatic façades which reached an extreme under William Butterfield at Rugby School Chapel and Keble College, Oxford. Some consider Manchester Town Hall (1869) to be Waterhouse's finest work. Here he adopts the Early English transitional style with more than a hint of Canterbury Cathedral Trinity Chapel. In some respects towns identified themselves as champions of the Gothic cause by adopting the style for their town hall. Chester and Northampton are notable examples, whereas others like Leeds and Bolton adopted the classical.

108   Prudential Assurance Building, Holborn, London. Alfred Waterhouse, 1878. One of the earliest purpose-built office blocks, in red brick and pink terracotta.

109 Bangor, Penrhyn Castle, 1827-40.

The Victorian age saw the last widespread building of the great houses finally rendered obsolete by the First World War. Subsequently, many have been demolished including Waterhouse's Eaton Hall, Cheshire. A popular period for reproduction was the Elizabethan, seen in Barry's Highclere Castle, Hants. (1842-4), and Anthony Salvin's Harlaxton Manor, Lincs. (1831-55), which verges on the Jacobean with Flemish gables and strapwork. Some patrons preferred the more conventional medieval manor layout reproducing another Penshurst or Haddon. Barry does this

110 North Oxford Gothic, Norham Gardens, c. 1870.

successfully with Canford Manor, Dorset (1848-52). At a
slightly more eccentric extreme is Penrhyn Castle near
Bangor by Thomas Hopper, in the Norman style with a keep
based on that of Rochester – Hopper's birthplace. The
great hall is derived from the nave of Durham Cathedral.

At a humbler level the Middle Ages inspired the red-
brick houses of the rapidly forming suburbs of large towns.
William Morris's Red House, Bexleyheath designed by
Philip Webb in 1859, was influential in forming a style
which combined sash windows, hipped gables and projected
porches to evoke the Gothic in upper-middle-class housing
in Ealing or North Oxford, yet providing the solid comforts
of Victorian life. With John Ruskin's *The Stones of Venice* the
revival could take yet another turn in England. More than a
slight trace of Venetian Gothic finds its way into warehouses
in Bristol – appropriately reflected in the dock basins – as
well as into commercial buildings in Liverpool, reaching a
climax in Templeton's Carpet Factory of 1889 in Glasgow.

Apart from the Gothic and its offshoots, the classical
must be seen as the other dominant style of this era,
although mention should first be made of the Oriental.
Chambers's Pagoda at Kew marks the arrival of the Chinese

*111   Brighton, Sussex, Royal
Pavilion, c. 1820. John Nash's
brilliant creation combining Hindu,
semi-Gothic and Classical elements.
The building was originally a neo-
classical villa by Henry Holland.*

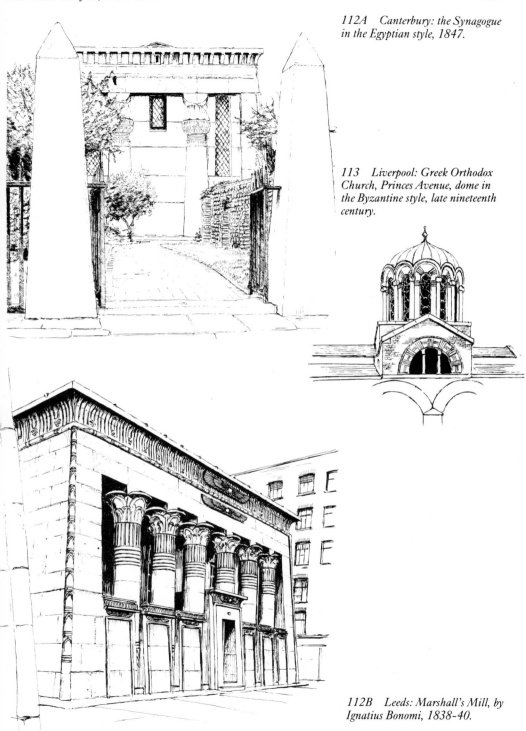

112A   Canterbury: the Synagogue in the Egyptian style, 1847.

113   Liverpool: Greek Orthodox Church, Princes Avenue, dome in the Byzantine style, late nineteenth century.

112B   Leeds: Marshall's Mill, by Ignatius Bonomi, 1838-40.

114   Westminster Cathedral,
begun in 1895. The result of the
dream of John Francis Bentley to
create a Byzantine church in
London. Although the inspiration
may at first appear to be Hagia
Sophia, Constantinople, the
handling of the domes on
pendentives rising from tall piers is
similar to that in St Mark's,
Venice. The inclusion of marble
arcading is also Venetian.

fashion in England which quickly spread to the Continent. The 'Hindoo' style arrived with Sezincote House, Glos. (1803), by Samuel Cockerell. Repton proposed a similar idea for the Prince Regent at Brighton, and further inspired by Coleridge's *Kubla Khan* in 1816, John Nash was able to create an oriental wonderland in Sussex for his 'Prince of Pleasure'. In fact the Royal Pavilion is a mixture of Indian domes, minarets, semi-Gothic arches and Moorish 'cast-iron' tracery, clothing Holland's neo-classical villa.

Even more original and exotic is the Egyptian fashion used for Marshall's Woollen Mill in Leeds from 1842, with obelisks serving as chimneys. The Canterbury Synagogue of about the same date is another fine attempt in this style. The Byzantine also made an appearance in both industrial and ecclesiastical building. Two examples of the latter are the Greek Orthodox Church, Princes Avenue, Liverpool from about 1880, and J.F. Bentley's Roman Catholic Cathedral at Westminster.

The English Baroque and Adam styles

The classical style in architecture went through a number of interpretations during the eighteenth and nineteenth centuries. The period opened with the so-called English Baroque at the hands of Hawksmoor, Vanbrugh, Talman and Thomas Archer. Apart from the great houses, remote from most of the population, the Baroque inspired a number of impressive town churches especially as a result of the Act of 1711 for 'Fifty New Churches in London and Westminster and the suburbs thereof'. Hawksmoor designed six which are highly personal interpretations of classical elements – and even Gothic, as in the spire of Christ Church, Spitalfields. They look somewhat forbidding in their weight of white Portland stone, yet show his feeling for scholarship as at St George, Bloomsbury, with its tower based on Pliny's account of the Tomb of Mausolus at Halicarnassus, or St Alfege, Greenwich, with Roman altars fronting the east portico.

115A   St George, Bloomsbury, 1716-31.

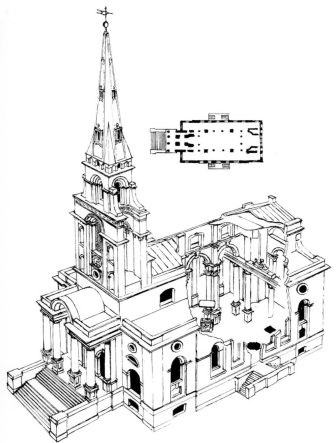

115B   Christ Church, Spitalfields, by Hawksmoor, 1714-29. As it appeared before alterations in the nineteenth century.

116A   London. St John's, Smith Square, Westminster. Thomas Archer, c. 1720.

116B   Tower of S. Agnese in the Piazza Navona, Rome by Borromini, c. 1652. The influence on Archer's towers is quite obvious.

116C   Birmingham, St Philip by Thomas Archer, c. 1709-16.

Even more Baroque in feeling are the three churches of Thomas Archer (1668-1743). Unlike Hawksmoor he had visited Rome and so had an intimate knowledge of Bernini's and Borromini's works. His towers on St John, Smith Square, Westminster, follow closely those of Borromini's S. Agnese in the Piazza Navona. At St Paul, Deptford, he breaks the block-like appearance by a semi-circular western portico, perhaps inspired by Bramante's Doric *tempietto* and Cortona's Sta Maria della Pace. The tower and steeple are circular and decorated with volutes and urns. His earliest church, St Philip, Birmingham (now the Cathedral) has a western tower which exploits Borromini's use of concave surfaces. Baroque influence is also found in the churches of James Gibbs, especially St Mary-le-Strand, also with a semi-circular western portico. The tower is strongly influenced by his mentor, Wren. At nearby St Martin-in-the-Fields the feeling is more Palladian with a western hexastyle portico and eastern Venetian window. The surrounds to windows consist of the alternating large and small blocks of stone known as a 'Gibbs surround'. The influence of Gibbs can be seen in provincial church building such as Wolverhampton, Worcester and Mereworth, Kent.

James Gibbs may be considered the bridge between English Baroque and Palladianism, the movement trying to rediscover the lost rules of Vitruvius. Robert Adam (1728-92) on the other hand, whilst sympathetic to the Palladian cause, could see its limitations and brought a new freedom of classical interpretation to England which the more academic architects such as Sir William Chambers could only describe as 'frivolous'. The son of William Adam, the leading Scottish architect of the day, Robert spent nearly four years in Rome with the French architect Clérisseau.

117   London, St Martin in the Fields, c. 1726. In it James Gibbs uses a mixture of Palladian and Baroque elements. The windows display the so-called Gibbs surround.

WEST FRONT HEXASTYLE PORTICO

He also surveyed the remains of Diocletian's palace at Split in Dalmatia and so was able at first hand to explore the variety of antique Roman domestic ornament. Back in England he set up as an extremely successful architect. He argued that the Romans used more freedom in design than hitherto known, and therefore one should not be restricted by a series of unbreakable rules. The architect should interpret anew according to the nature of his commission.

Adam's ornamentation, based on a number of sources not all purely Classical, introduced a new visual alphabet. He was essentially an interior architect and a master in the conversion or completion of houses started by other architects. Much of his ornament was in shallow plaster relief in gilt or contrasting pastel shades. Favourite motifs include arabesques, anthemion (honeysuckle) flowers, Greek-key or fret, Vitruvian scroll, egg-and-leaf and dart. Ceilings were divided into geometrical patterns with occasionally painted panels of antique pastoral subjects by Angelica Kauffmann. Columns and pilasters were usually of alabaster, or scagliola, a material composed of cement or plaster and marble chips and coloured to imitate marble; although in the Ante-room of Syon House he actually used antique columns dredged from the Tiber. During the 1770s he became, along with the potter Josiah Wedgwood, the chief exponent of the 'Etruscan' fashion based on the reddish-brown, black, and yellow colour schemes of early Greek vases, which were then thought to be the work of the Etruscan civilization stamped out by the Romans. The best example of this phase of Adam is the Etruscan Room at Osterley House.

Kedleston Hall from 1761 expresses the range of Adam's virtuosity as a designer. It had been started as a Palladian mansion by James Paine; Adam took over and created the columned hall strongly reminiscent of Burlington's York Assembly Room. Beyond is a circular salon with a coffered dome based on the Roman Pantheon. The South Front exhibits a strong triumphal-arch motif derived from the Arch of Constantine and Nicolo Salvi's Trevi Fountain of about 1735, which Adam knew from his years in Rome. The interior retains a succession of magnificent rooms; especially notable are the dining room and music room, both with ceiling decorations based on recently excavated motifs from Pompeii. Both Syon and Osterley were conversions of older houses; at the former the library is converted from a Jacobean long gallery with book cases set into the wall between pilasters. At Osterley almost all of one side of the quadrangular-planned house was demolished to make way for a large double portico derived partly from the Propylaea at Athens, and partly from the Temple of the Sun at Palmyra. Adam's numerous other works range from the

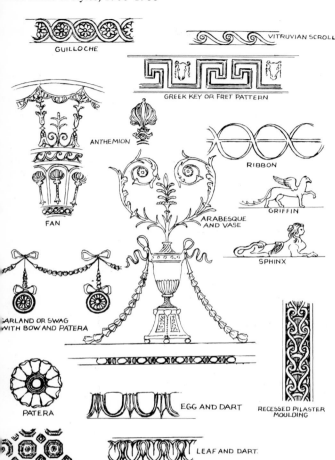

118 *Adam ornamental motifs.*

GUILLOCHE

VITRUVIAN SCROLL

GREEK KEY OR FRET PATTERN

ANTHEMION

RIBBON

GRIFFIN

FAN

ARABESQUE
AND VASE

SPHINX

GARLAND OR SWAG
WITH BOW AND PATERA

PATERA

EGG AND DART

RECESSED PILASTER
MOULDING

LEAF AND DART

COFFERING

interior of Home House, 20 Portman Square, London (1773-7) to Charlotte Square and the University at Edinburgh.

Adam's closest followers, or 'plagiarists' as some would claim, were James Wyatt (1746-1813), better known for his Gothic restoration and Fonthill, and Thomas Leverton (1743-1824), whose Etruscan rooms at Woodhall Park, Herts., equal those of Adam.

The Greek Revival 1790-1830

A few years before Adam set up in practice in London a profound revolution of historical thought struck the world of art and archaeology. The German art historian Johann Winckelmann produced his *Reflections on the Paintings and Sculpture of the Greeks* in Dresden in 1755, in which he

119   *Kedleston Hall, Derby, from
1761. South front by Robert Adam
showing its derivation from Arch of
Constantine c. 300 (left) and Trevi
Fountain c. 1735 (right), both in
Rome.*

proclaimed the Greek civilization as the basis of the
Classical ideal and therefore of European culture. This had
the immediate effect of inspiring architects and travellers to
seek genuine Greek remains, in Greece and southern Italy.
The first Englishman to take up this challenge was James
'Athenian' Stuart, who, having spent 1751-3 in Greece,
built a Doric temple in the grounds of Hagley Hall, Worcs.,
in 1758. His book *The Antiquities of Athens* appeared in 1762
but the Greek revival in England did not get fully underway
until the 1790s, by which time its qualities were being
expounded also in Paris and Berlin.

When it did blossom the Greek revival was but one aspect
of the romantic vision of the virtues of a past golden age. So
potent was the vision that Edinburgh New Town became an
attempt to create an 'Athens in the North'. William
Hamilton's Royal High School in part copies the Theseum

120   *Edinburgh, Royal High
School. Thomas Hamilton's
building, 1826-9, inspired by the
Theseum, Athens.*

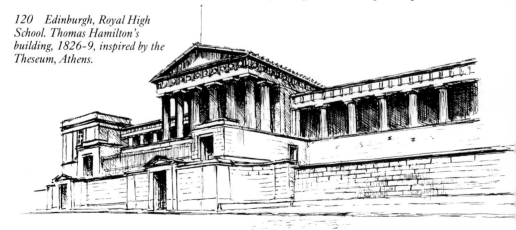

at Athens. On the Calton Hill behind stand gigantic fluted Doric columns from the unfinished project to reproduce the Parthenon as a memorial to the dead of the Napoleonie Wars.

One of its most enthusiastic supporters was William Wilkins (1778-1839) whose two major London works, University College and the National Gallery, feature the Corinthian order and tall central porticoes. At Cambridge Wilkins designed Downing College where each block incorporates Ionic porticoes derived from the Erechtheum which is also the major source for St Pancras Church by H. and W. Inwood (1819-22). The famous caryatids are also copied on the north and south sides and the tower is inspired by the Athenian Tower of the Winds. Appropriately the major museums of the early nineteenth

121   Liverpool. Former St James's Cemetery. Mortuary chapel in the Greek Doric style, c. 1820. Full use is made of the site on the edge of an eighteenth-century quarry.

century were in the Greek style, including Sir Robert Smirke's British Museum with its impressive south front of 48 Ionic columns, and the Ashmolean in Oxford by C. R. Cockerell, again featuring Ionic columns.

Gradually the Greek fashion seemed, like the Gothic, to find its way into many areas of building, from banks to gentlemen's clubs, and was even adopted by railway companies. Euston Station was adorned with a huge Doric arch by Philip Hardwick to mark the terminus of the London and Birmingham Railway in 1838, whilst in Birmingham, Curzon Street Station remains, with its Ionic façade.

The Regency 1810-37
Although George Prince of Wales was only Regent from 1810 to 1820 the term Regency for artistic purposes is usually applied to the period 1810-37. Dominated at one end by magnificent buildings of stone reflecting the Greek fashion, it was also the age when 'stucco' came into its own

123   Cheltenham, Glos. Caryatid in plaster.

122   London, St Pancras Church, 1819-21. London's purest essay in the Greek style.

124   *Canterbury. Regency bow-fronted house, brick with stucco face,* c. *1820.*

125   *Greenwich. Typical Regency bowed bay on garden front.*

to reproduce grandeur on the cheap. The age is dominated
by John Nash and his development of London's West End
to rival Napoleon's Paris. The layout of Regent's Park with
its terraces, Regent Street, and Carlton House Terrace
were commissions larger than any given to any other English
architect until modern times.

Much of Nash's work is brick, faced only on the visible
façades with stucco. With his 'penchant' for columns which
gave a façade additional visual definition and strength he
used even cast iron as in those at the foot of Carlton House
Terrace on the Mall side. Nash's Regent Street façades
have been destroyed, but his great Regent's Park's terraces
survive and look like palaces when viewed from across the
park.

The development of inland spas started in the eighteenth
century and whilst this continued especially at Cheltenham,
the middle and working classes discovered the sea. Many
resorts grew at this time with small stucco-fronted hotels
and lodging houses with a little added classical pretence
here and there, such as classical pilasters, bow-fronted bays
and wrought-iron balconies. There are resorts too
numerous to mention, but they include Brighton, Margate,
Weymouth, Hastings and Sidmouth on the south coast and
Scarborough and Tynemouth on the east.

XIX

Nineteenth-century industrial architecture

Historians will never agree as to exactly when the Industrial Revolution began; some will make a case for the age of cannon in the sixteenth-century Weald of Sussex, others put it as late as after 1830 with the development of steam power for rail and water transport. Artists such as Wright of Derby and de Loutherbourg were inspired by the furnaces of Coalbrookdale in the 1770s.

The Great Iron Bridge built there in 1779 by Abraham Darby may be said to mark a revolution in architectural design. The fine parallel arch ribs 100 feet in length help to span a river gorge which would have hitherto required a huge viaduct. The roadway rests on iron plates. As the years of the nineteenth century passed so methods of iron smelting were improved and designers saw the increasing advantages of cast iron in building, none more so than Thomas Telford (1757-1834).

Telford's greatest works include the magnificent Pont Cysylltau Aqueduct which carried the Shropshire Union

127   *Coalbrookdale, Salop. Iron Bridge, 1779.*

128   Clifton Suspension Bridge,
I.K. Brunel. Over three hundred
feet above the river Avon, it cut a
seven-mile road journey between
Clifton, and Leigh in Somerset to a
few hundred yards.

129   Chester. Suspension Bridge
across the Dee, built in 1852 and
reconstructed in 1923.

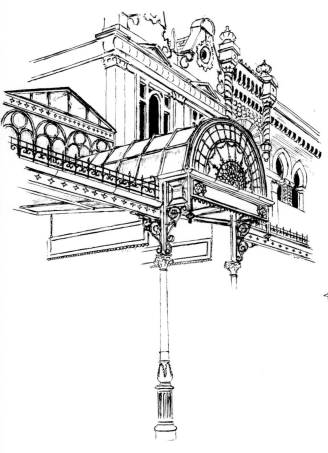

131   Southport, Merseyside. Cast-iron shopping arcade, 1898. The Moorish influence in the façade behind is worthy of note.

130   Greenwich. Wrought iron bandstand in Greenwich Park, c. 1880.

Canal over the River Dee in the Vale of Llangollen, with cast iron segmented arches supported by huge masonry piers nearly 130 feet high. Another equally magnificent work is his Menai Straits Suspension Bridge (1820-6), linking Anglesey with north Wales, one of the earliest of its kind. Telford's rival Isambard Kingdom Brunel designed the Clifton Suspension Bridge over the most dramatic scenery, the Avon gorge near Bristol. The principle of the suspension bridge was quickly assimilated, whereby the chains from which the roadway was suspended were anchored at each end into brick or stone pylons reinforced by cast iron. It soon led to a fashion for such bridges over shallow rivers and park lakes, along with cast iron bandstands, palm houses, circular restaurants or rotundas, and shopping arcades.

With the development of larger ships and an increasing export and import market, riverside quays for unloading were no longer sufficient, since ships would block the river

132   Liverpool, Albert Dock,
1841-5. Jesse Hartley and Philip
Hardwick.
The warehouses are carried on
massive Doric cast-iron columns, a
feature which Hartley also used in
the nearby Wapping and Stanley
docks.

passage. Docks had been dug for the building and repair of
naval ships at Portsmouth and Chatham in the seventeenth
century, whilst at Liverpool the 'Old Dock' was dug in 1715
to begin the phenomenal rise of this merchant port. Further
docks were opened there before the first dock in London,
the West India, was opened in 1802. Docks were quickly
linked by brick warehouses which over the course of the
nineteenth century adopted various styles of architecture
from the Romanesque to the Italianate classical. Many were
the largest single buildings so far created and have a unique
grandeur of their own. Unfortunately Telford's and
Hardwick's St Katharine's Dock warehouses, with their
cast-iron Doric columns forming ground colonnades, have
been partially demolished; however at Albert Dock,
Liverpool, the five-storey warehouses of 1841-5 still
surround the four sides of the dock with cast-iron
colonnades. At Stanley Dock the Tobacco Warehouse from
1900, built of red and blue brick above a high rusticated
stone base, rises to eleven storeys and is said to be the largest
in the world. Besides warehouses other architectural
features of note in docks include gateways, watchmen's
huts, dockmasters' houses, and hydraulic towers which at
Liverpool are gently affected by the Gothic.

*133   Liverpool, Stanley Dock
Tobacco Warehouse, 1900. The
Gothic Hydraulic Tower on the left
from 1848 is worthy of note.*

With the railway revolution all styles were exploited to the full and rules broken if necessary. Whilst the London and Birmingham Railway adopted the Classical for its railway stations, the Great Western used Gothic at Temple Meads, Bristol, and Jacobean at Paddington. The Tudor was a favourite style for country railway stations with tall gabled walls and chimneys. Tunnel mouths came in all kinds, including Gothic at Bramhope, and Classical at Box in Wilts. and Watford, Herts. Bridges and viaducts are also of considerable architectural splendour yet are rarely noticed by the traveller. Sometimes they followed set stylistic requirements of a particular railway company or designer. For instance, Brunel insisted that all bridges between Bath and Bristol on the Great Western should have pointed arches.

Cast iron as a frame for glazing a wide area was perhaps first used by Thomas Hopper for a conservatory at Carlton House for the Prince of Wales in 1807. It was exploited on a

*134   Liverpool, Sandon Dock.
Ornamental dock gate incorporating
keeper's hut, 1848.*

*135 Bramhope Tunnel,
Yorkshire. North Portal in
castellated Gothic for Leeds and
Thirsk Railway Co., c. 1840.*

*136 Box, Wilts. Western portal
of tunnel on former Great Western
Railway. It has the flavour of a
classical arch; c. 1840.*

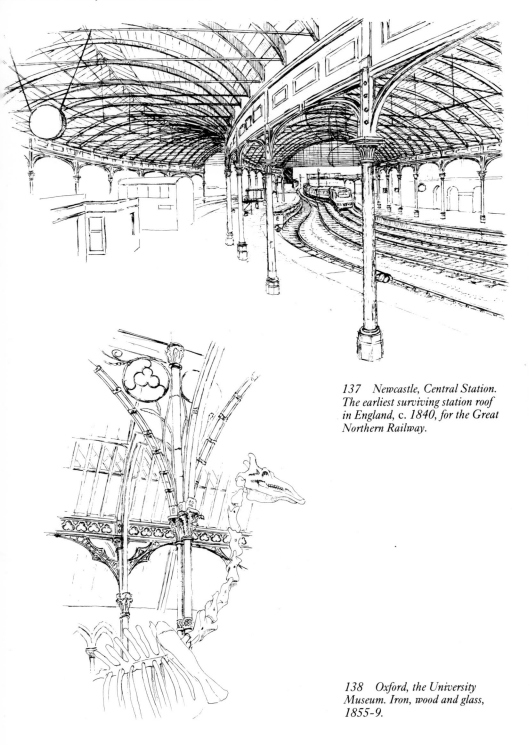

137   Newcastle, Central Station.
The earliest surviving station roof
in England, c. 1840, for the Great
Northern Railway.

138   Oxford, the University
Museum. Iron, wood and glass,
1855-9.

larger scale by Joseph Paxton in his Conservatory at Chatsworth, and the Crystal Palace, Hyde Park, for the 1851 Great Exhibition. It was obvious that a wide span was essential for a train shed and so iron and glass was quickly adopted for major station roofing; the earliest surviving example is Newcastle Central (1846-55), where it rests on two rows of iron pillars which follow the long curve of the tracks. Cast iron and glass can also be seen providing an effective contrast to the skeletal exhibits in the Oxford Museum.

As society became more industrialized, new types of buildings developed: gas works, power stations, water pumping houses, tram depots and specialist factories and mills. Many of these are being preserved where possible and provide an interesting variety of design, often drawn from the most unlikely origins. Could any fifteenth-century Venetian ever dream that his palaces with their swallow-tail battlements might provide inspiration for a nineteenth-century carpet factory in Glasgow?

The Industrial Revolution saw the spread of vast areas of cheap terraced housing for the working population, often thrown up without regard to health or aesthetic considerations. All Britain's great industrial cities contain such areas – Leeds, Manchester and Liverpool are good examples. The development of the terraced house is looked at more closely in the next chapter.

139   Durham: railway viaduct c. 1846 in stone rising above late nineteenth century brick terraces which climb the steep sides of the Wear Valley.

XX

The twentieth century

It is hard to make any general judgement on the architectural fashions of this century when each decade has brought radical change. No previous century has seen such massive urban development, and also destruction brought by war. Many provincial town centres have been gutted since the war in a 'cycle of urban renewal', bringing in some cases a totally new street plan and skyline dominated by huge tower blocks.

Before the beginning of the century towns were divided into social areas by their architecture. Industry often led to cramped planning with rows of identical terraced blocks facing each other across treeless streets. The simplest façades were flat, although a minor relief of monotony might be a projecting window bay for the front sitting room. As the

140   Highpoint I, Highgate, 1935, Tecton Group. This block on the heights to the north of London marked a revolutionary advance in luxury flat design. Influenced by continental development and in particular the work of Le Corbusier, its clean and simple lines are reinforced by the pattern of lit and shadowed surfaces. Le Corbusier called it the 'world's first vertical city'.

social scale rose, a small front garden might appear along with the introduction of contrasting coloured brick or stone. In the most densely populated areas tenement blocks were erected by voluntary housing trusts, such as those remaining in Stepney and Southwark, London, by the Peabody Trust. Further up the social scale the 'Queen Anne' style with varied brick and terracotta broken by carefully proportioned sash windows became popular with Norman Shaw (1831-1912), one of its best exponents. For those who could afford to live in the country, a variety of domestic styles could be adapted to their needs by Shaw, from the late medieval half-timbered manor to eighteenth-century Georgian such as Bryanston, Dorset. Sir Edwin Lutyens (1869-1944) was equally inventive in his adaptation of past styles, especially Georgian, employing where possible local materials. He built a number of important houses, which were not slavish imitations of the past but original in his use of detail, before the First World War brought social and economic changes and the demand for smaller properties. Perhaps his Castle Drogo in Devon from about 1910 was the last new country house in England. One of his best Georgian works is 'The Salutation', Sandwich, from 1911.

In the early years of this century the Baroque also received a revival, although within the constraints of the English temperament, which favoured a weighty grandeur rather than a multiplicity of curving and broken surfaces. Certainly the Norwich Union building in Norwich by C.J. Skipper owes more to Vanbrugh than to Borromini, indeed the use of arches and heavy rusticated stonework is reminiscent of Seaton Delaval. The Baroque style was also chosen for a number of impressive civic buildings. Probably the grandest in the style are those composing the Cardiff Civic Centre incorporating many characteristic elements including a tall tower, and the dome on the Town Hall block at the centre of the huge layout. The firm of Lanchester, Stewart and Rickards were responsible for this project between about 1897 and 1908, as well as the much smaller Baroque town hall at Deptford, started in 1902. At nearby Woolwich, the town hall has a tower which is quite obviously derived from Wren's western towers of St Paul's, and Borromini's S. Agnese, in Rome. After the First World War the Baroque lost its popularity as a style for public buildings; indeed its greatest exposition, the Roman Catholic Cathedral for Liverpool by Lutyens in the 1930s, never got above ground level. Only the giant crypt was built before the Second World War brought work to a standstill. With the architect's death in 1944, the drive to keep the plan alive during the period of post-war austerity was lacking, and so the building of a cathedral almost to rival St Peter's, Rome, in size was abandoned.

Back in 1850 Sir Titus Salt had set up a cloth mill on the banks of the Aire near Shipley, around which he built homes for his employees, as well as a chapel, hospital, high school and School of Art. This idea of healthy spacious living conditions was taken up by other industrialists such as George Cadbury at Bournville, and Lord Leverhulme at Port Sunlight. Under the impetus of Ebenezer Howard the Garden City Association was formed in order to halt the ever-increasing sprawl of large cities. This resulted in Hampstead Garden Suburb (partly by Lutyens) and also Letchworth, and Welwyn, both in Herts. After the Second World War more new towns were set up, ranging from Harlow to Skelmersdale near Liverpool.

The Garden City did not halt the sprawl of towns but rather provided goals at which the ribbon development could aim, encouraged by the needs of the motor car age, symbolised perhaps by the Kingston bypass in Surrey. The age of the neat semi-detached brick house, partly rendered in mortar and sporting struts of black painted wood to look 'Elizabethan', had arrived along with the Austin Seven and the radio. It seemed that perhaps the only way to stop growing outwards was to build upwards.

Some observers would claim that until well into the 1920s British architects were too conservative and closely bound to historical movements to break new ground, with the exploration of the full potential of modern materials. Pioneering advances in construction techniques were made in Germany just before the First World War by such designers as Walter Gropius, Peter Behrens, and from the 1920s, Eric Mendelsohn. This, the so-called International Modern style, was characterised by a rejection of unnecessary ornament so that the exterior of a building should express its inner function. Plain surfaces, large windows set within steel frames, and flat roofs, and often a reliance on white surfaces of concrete or painted brick were the keynote of this severely Cubist style. The first building in Britain to show some of the elements of the style, or Movement, was 'New Ways', Northampton, designed by Peter Behrens in 1925. Whilst right-angles were a predominant Cubist feature, the curve was not abandoned. Erich Mendelsohn, who left Germany in 1933, worked for a time in England, where his best-known work is the De La Warr Pavilion at Bexhill of 1935-7. Here he introduced a semicircular glazed stair tower: he had exploited curves in his Einstein Tower at Potsdam in 1919-20. Gropius also came to England, and collaborated with Maxwell Fry on the Impingham Village College in Cambridgeshire in 1935-7. This became the inspiration for much post-Second World

141   Liverpool waterfront.
Liver Building (left, 1908-11), by
Aubrey Thomas – one of the world's
first reinforced-concrete office
blocks; former Cunard office, now
Customs House (centre, 1915-18),
by W.E. Willinke and P.C.
Thicknesse, in the style of an Italian
Renaissance palazzo; Mersey Docks
and Harbour Board building
(right, 1903-7), by Arnold
Thornley, in the Italian Baroque.

War school building where the emphasis was on a light and spacious classroom environment. The International style had a limited effect on English domestic architecture, being largely confined to professional middle-class patrons, mostly in the southern counties.

The trend to build upwards was started under the influence of the International Style and the vision of cities climbing hundreds of feet into the sky as expounded by Le Corbusier, and Mies van der Rohe. The former's Unité d'Habitation in Marseilles, 1946-52, supported on thin pilotis (pillars) can easily be seen as the inspiration for many huge blocks of flats which have arisen throughout Britain in the 1960s and 1970s, though the trend to high-rise domestic blocks had actually started in London with Highpoint 1 at Highgate, 1933-5 by the firm of Tecton. This block provided a radical break with the horizontal balconied flats of the 1930s such as Quarry Hill, Leeds.

By the 1970s the 'high rise' block was seen to produce many socially undesirable effects from isolation to rising rates of crime, consequently we can see today a return to low-rise development.

142 *London, Centrepoint.
Richard Seifert 1962-5. As a
tower block it has considerable
beauty but with its height would be
more at home dominating a new
Spanish coastal resort rather than
the locality of St Giles Circus, with
its mixture of eighteenth- and
nineteenth-century streets. The
church in the foreground is St Giles
in the Fields, by Henry Flitcroft,
opened in 1734.*

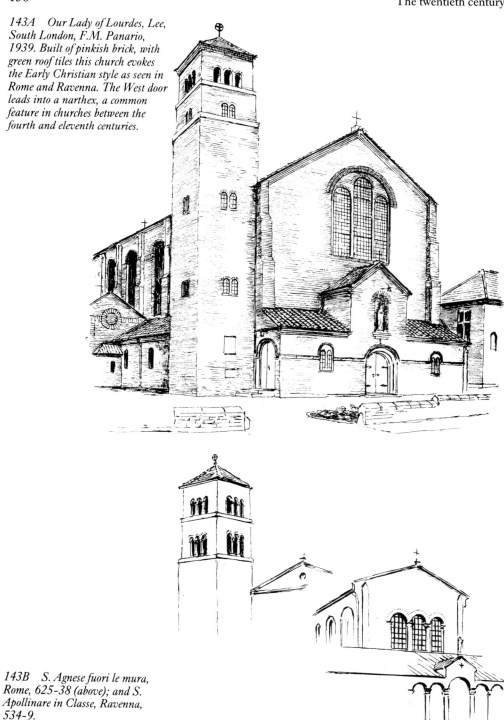

143A   Our Lady of Lourdes, Lee, South London, F.M. Panario, 1939. Built of pinkish brick, with green roof tiles this church evokes the Early Christian style as seen in Rome and Ravenna. The West door leads into a narthex, a common feature in churches between the fourth and eleventh centuries.

143B   S. Agnese fuori le mura, Rome, 625-38 (above); and S. Apollinare in Classe, Ravenna, 534-9.

144   Battersea Power Station, 1931, Sir Giles Gilbert Scott's masterpiece in which he proved that even an industrial building could be graceful. The chimneys rise like fluted columns.

With the coming of the railway, city centres changed from being domestic to largely commercial centres. The office block had become an object of considerable architectural pretention, as seen at the Prudential Assurance office in Holborn, 1878. Style could be conventionally Renaissance or Baroque, or 'modern', rejecting all previous fashions. Changing technology, particularly the increasing use of steel-frame construction, encouraged innovation. At the Kodak Building, Kingsway, London, 1911, the steel frames are revealed but at the Royal Liver Building, Liverpool, 1908-11 they are hidden within the reinforced concrete and the stonework of the Baroque façades. The latter provides a magnificent contrast to the neighbouring Cunard Offices in the style of an Italian Renaissance palace, and the Mersey Docks and Harbour Board offices with its Baroque domes. On the other hand Ronald Ward's Vickers Tower on Millbank, London, from the early 1960s was built with sufficient confidence to reject historicism and exploit to the full the effect of concave and convex glass surfaces held together with the minimum of steel framing. It seems a more pleasing solution to tower block design than Mies van der Rohe's Seagram Building in New York of 1956-8, and by reaching to a height of 387 feet, was the first building in London to exceed that of St Paul's. It was soon followed by

145   *Coventry Cathedral,*
1954-9. Opinion will forever be
divided as to whether the medieval
cathedral should have been restored,
or whether the new building provides
a satisfying visual alternative.

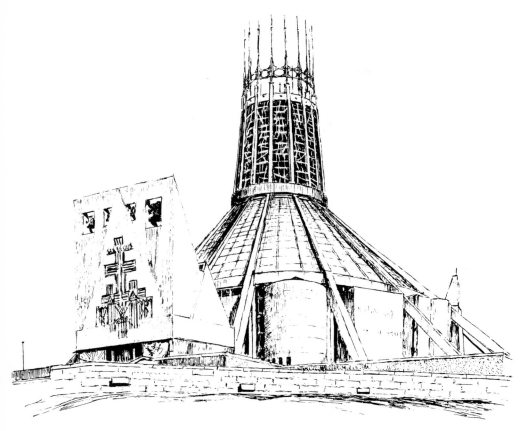

146   Liverpool, Roman Catholic Cathedral, 1962-7.

other commercial tower blocks including the controversial Centrepoint, and the National Westminster Tower in the City, over 600 feet in height, both by Richard Seifert.

Though we may be in full agreement with the critics who condemn the 'City of Towers' as twentieth-century 'environmental brutalism', this century has also proved that functional architecture can be beautiful, such as Battersea Power Station by Sir Giles Gilbert Scott (1929-46). Built of a pinkish brick with white fluted chimneys, it is almost as well loved as St Paul's Cathedral. Other brick masterpieces, although on a much smaller scale, are some of the London Underground Stations of the 1930s, and even those 'cathedrals of entertainment', the cinemas of the 1930s, glazed in black and ivory tiles on the outside, could offer Baroque extravagance within, as at the Astoria, Finsbury Park, of 1930.

Perhaps as our story began with churches it might end
with them. The twentieth century has seen architects look
back into the past for inspiration such as to sixth-century
Italy at Our Lady of Lourdes, Lee, London (1939); the
Gothic with the nave of Downside Abbey and Liverpool
Anglican Cathedral, both by Scott; and with Guildford
Cathedral by Sir Edward Maufe, 1936. At Coventry, by Sir
Basil Spence (started in 1954) we may see a more original
approach to cathedral planning with the walls angled to
project the light towards the altar. Since architecture, like all
visual arts, is ultimately a matter of personal judgement and
taste, some may feel that Frederick Gibberd's Metropolitan
Roman Catholic Cathedral at Liverpool with its altar set in
the centre of the circular plan brings one closer to the centre
of worship than the long nave of a medieval cathedral, and
therefore marks the direction of church planning for the
future.

Appendix: Cities and towns of major architectural interest

This list is limited to those places which exhibit many buildings of interest, both secular and ecclesiastical, and which retain a character typical of their geographical location. It should be stressed that those offering considerable scope for architectural study are not necessarily allied with natural surroundings of the same distinction. Nor are the most interesting architectural examples to be found in the main thoroughfares. Often the side streets and even alleys bring their reward. A seemingly unimpressive nineteenth-century façade may, on close examination, prove to be a mask for a much older structure, possibly even medieval. This is especially the case in such cities as Canterbury and York and owners are frequently most helpful in allowing the keen student to see the hidden façade at the back as well as providing useful historical information. The best handbooks for a study of specific locations are those in the Buildings of England series edited by Nikolaus Pevsner. The Royal Commission on Historical Monuments (H.M.S.O.) have also published scholarly reports on a number of places, and although many are out of print they may be consulted in good reference libraries (see Bibliography).

AVON
  Bath
  Bristol

BEDS
  Bedford
  Dunstable

BERKS
  Faringdon

BUCKS
  Beaconsfield
  Buckingham
  Marlow
  Wendover
  West Wycombe

CAMBS
  Cambridge
  Ely
  Newmarket
  St Neots
  Wisbech

CHESHIRE
  Chester

Congleton
Nantwich
Sandbach

CORNWALL
  Helston
  Launceston
  Penzance
  St Ives
  Truro

CUMBRIA
  Carlisle
  Kendal
  Keswick

DERBY
  Ashbourne
  Bakewell
  Buxton
  Matlock
  Repton

DEVON
  Barnstable
  Brixham

Crediton
Exeter
Okehampton
Sidmouth
Teignmouth
Totnes

DORSET
  Bournemouth
  Blandford
  Christchurch
  Dorchester
  Shaftesbury
  Sherborne
  Weymouth
  Wimborne

DURHAM
  Barnard Castle
  Chester-le-Street
  Durham

ESSEX
  Colchester
  Dedham
  Maldon

Saffron Walden
Thaxted

GLOS
Cheltenham
Chipping Camden
Cirencester
Fairford
Gloucester
Northleach
Tetbury
Tewkesbury
Winchcomb

HANTS
Lymington
Portsmouth
Romsey
Southampton
Winchester

HEREFORDSHIRE
Great Malvern
Hereford
Ledbury

HERTFORDSHIRE
Bishops Stortford
Hertford
Royston

HUMBERSIDE
Beverley

KENT
Canterbury
Charing
Cranbrook
Faversham
Goudhurst
Lamberhurst
Maidstone
Rochester
Sandwich
Sevenoaks
Tenterden
Tunbridge Wells
Westerham

LANCS
Clitheroe
Lancaster

LEICS
Market Harborough
Melton Mowbray
Oakham
Uppingham

LINCS
Boston
Gainsborough
Grantham
Lincoln
Louth
Stamford

LONDON
Cities of London,
and Westminster
Blackheath
Charlton
Chiswick
Dulwich
Greenwich
Hampstead
Highgate
Islington
Limehouse
Southwark
Spitalfields
Woolwich

MANCHESTER
Manchester
and Salford
Bolton

MERSEYSIDE
Liverpool
Port Sunlight
Southport

NORFOLK
East Dereham
King's Lynn
Norwich
Thetford
Wymondham

NORTHANTS
Higham Ferrers
Oundle
Rushden

NORTHUMBERLAND
Alnwick
Berwick
Morpeth
Newcastle (Tyne and Wear)
Rothbury

NOTTS
Newark
Nottingham
Worksop

OXON
Abingdon
Burford
Henley
Oxford
Wallingford
Wantage
Witney
Woodstock

SALOP
Bridgenorth
Church Stretton
Ludlow
Shrewsbury

SOMERSET
Bridgewater
Dunster
Ilminster
Street
Taunton
Wells

SUFFOLK
Aldeburgh
Bury St Edmunds
Clare
Kersey
Lavenham
Long Melford
Needham Market
Southwold

SURREY
Farnham
Guildford
Kew
Reigate
Richmond

SUSSEX
Arundel
Brighton
Chichester
East Grinstead
Lewes
Midhurst
Petworth
Rye
Steyning
Winchelsea

STAFFS
Lichfield

WARWICKS
  Coventry
  Henley in Arden
  Leamington
  Stratford on Avon
  Warwick

WILTS
  Bradford on Avon
  Calne
  Malmesbury

Marlborough
Salisbury
Wilton

WORCS
  Broadway
  Evesham
  Malvern
  Stourbridge
  Worcester

YORKS
  Bradford

Beverley
Harrogate
Leeds
Malton
Richmond
Ripon
Scarborough
Selby
Skipton
Whitby
York

Practically every area of London has examples of architecture worthy of study. Her development may be seen as the growing together of many villages and small communities without any formal planning, and many suburbs still exhibit something of their rural character, such as Hampstead, Dulwich and Charlton. At the heart is the City which, although of Roman origin, has practically nothing surviving before 1600, apart from a few churches, the Charterhouse and the medieval walls – the Tower is outside the City boundary. Factors worthy of consideration when studying the architectural character of a district include surviving evidence of the original settlement, e.g. church, houses (usually of the wealthier classes), almshouses. In the last war some areas of London were severely damaged, and have suffered subsequent urban decay and major population shifts, yet in recent years, especially in South London, there has been some most successful restoration of late eighteenth- and early nineteenth-century housing, as in the Peckham, Camberwell, Kennington area. Other areas may be termed 'zones in transition', where their character has been radically altered by large-scale redevelopment. Spitalfields is an excellent example where early eighteenth-century terraces survive in close proximity to tall, concrete-and-glass flats of the 1970s. On the other hand, Covent Garden is a district where conservation groups fought successfully to preserve the largely nineteenth-century character against wholesale redevelopment. These areas are well worth a visit, but all the areas mentioned in the list below have their own interest from the architectural point of view.

Glossary

ABACUS
flat slab on top of a capital, usually square in classical and Romanesque, circular or oval in Gothic.

ABUTMENT
the solid part of a pier from which an arch springs. It can be used to describe the division of the arches within a bridge.

ACANTHUS
plant with thick scalloped leaves used as part of the decoration of a Corinthian capital.

AISLE
lateral portion of a church or cathedral parallel to the nave, choir, and chancel and separated from them by an arcade. Except in so-called hall churches, the aisles are usually much lower in height than the central nave etc., thus allowing for a clerestory.

ALCOVE
a recess in a room sometimes set aside for a bed.

ALMONRY
a building adjacent to a monastery in which alms were distributed to the poor.

ALMSHOUSE
a building devoted to the shelter of poor persons and often endowed by a rich benefactor such as a merchant. Some were for men or women of a specific social or professional background and were known as colleges, such as Morden College, Blackheath, and College of Matrons, Salisbury

AMBO
an elevated lectern or pulpit in the nave.

AMBULATORY
semi-circular or polygonal aisle enclosing an apse.

ANNULET
shaft-ring, found especially in Early English styles.

ANTHEMION
ornament based on the honeysuckle and frequently employed by Robert Adam and his followers.

APSE
a semicircular domed recess at the east end of chancels, or chapels, or against the east wall of a transept, the latter prevalent in Romanesque 'greater church' planning.

ARCADE
range of arches supported on piers or columns.

ARABESQUE
geometrical and complicated decoration, involving intertwined tendrils and foliage. Used by the Greeks and Romans, it was a favourite theme of Robert Adam.

AQUEDUCT
a bridge for conveying water across a lower level such as a valley. In England they were frequently built for canals with the water carried in a cast iron trough.

ARCHITRAVE	lowest of the three main parts of the entablature in classical architecture.
ASHLAR	cut stone worked to even faces and right-angled edges.
ATTIC	top storey of a house, in classical architecture it is often defined as such by a boldly projecting cornice at its base.
BAILEY	open space or court within the walls of a castle; often called a ward in late medieval castles.
BALDACCHINO	a canopy placed over an altar, supported on columns; a good modern example is that in St Paul's Cathedral, London.
BALL-FLOWER	a fourteenth-century decoration comprising a globular flower of three petals enclosing a small ball.
BALUSTRADE	series of balusters supporting a handrail or coping. Can be used to adorn a parapet or mark the divisions of a garden terrace.
BARBICAN	an outwork or defence before a fortified gate. Examples remain at Bodiam Castle, Sussex, and Lion Tower, Tower of London.
BARGE-BOARDS	overhanging decorated boards against the incline of the gable of a building. Many fine examples survive on half-timbered houses of the sixteenth century.
BAROQUE	the architecture of the seventeenth and early eighteenth centuries characterised by concave and convex wall surfaces. Sometimes the rules of classical proportions were deliberately distorted. Asymmetry was also a deliberate characteristic of Continental Baroque at its most extreme. In England the term is limited to building between about 1660 and 1730 at the hands of such architects as Wren, Hawksmoor, Vanbrugh, Talman, Archer, and Gibbs, and is muted by classical restraint, in comparison with the Italians, Bernini, Borromini and Guarini.
BASILICA	in medieval architecture an aisled church with clerestory. It originally had an apse at one end and was the basis of Early Christian church planning.
BASTION	projection at the angle of a fortification.
BATTLEMENT	parapet with a series of indentations or embrasures known as crenelles between raised portions or merlons. Such a parapet is described as being crenellated.
BAY	internal division of a building by piers or columns against the wall and transverse arches in ceiling or vault. See plans of Lincoln Cathedral and Westminster Abbey (Figures 11 and 18).
BAY-WINDOW	angular or curved projection of a house front.

BEAK-HEAD	Norman ornamental motif consisting of a row of grotesque bird or beast heads with beaks usually biting into the semi-circular or roll-moulded surround of the arch of a door or window.
BELFRY	upper stage of a tower where bells are hung.
BELLCOTE	framework of timber or stone on a roof from which to hang bells.
BLIND TRACERY	tracery purely for decorative purposes applied to walls without glazing or openings. Extensively used during the Norman and Early English periods.
BLOCK CAPITAL	(also called Cushion Capital). Romanesque capital cut from a cube by having the lower angles of each side rounded off to the circular shaft below.
BOSS	key stone at the meeting of vault ribs. It is usually decorated with figure or foliated carving (see Figure 14).
BRICKWORK	brick laid in courses according to specific patterns or bonds (see Figure 149).
BROACH	Early English spire generally octagonal in plan rising from the four sides of the tower. A small pyramidal piece of masonry covers the triangular space at each of the four corners – see Figure 27A.
BUTTRESS	stone or brick support projecting from a wall to give additional strength especially where the pressure of internal vaulting places stress against the interior surfaces (see Figure 11).
CABLE MOULDING	Norman moulding imitating rope or a twisted cord.
CAPITAL	carved or moulded block of stone placed on top of column.
CARTOUCHE	decorative tablet or frame for inscriptions or coat of arms.
CARYATID	whole female figure supporting an entablature.
CASTELLATED	battlemented.
CASTLE	a building fortified for defence. Usually of stone and flint, although towards the end of the Middle Ages a number were built of brick.
CHANCEL	part of church in which the altar is placed. It usually refers to the whole of the church east of the crossing.
CHANCEL ARCH	arch dividing chancel from nave.
CHANTRY CHAPEL	chapel attached to, or inside church endowed by a benefactor for the saying of mass for his soul and those of his family on specific feast days. A chantry bequest might include funds for the retaining of a priest for this purpose as well as teaching grammar to the local children.

CHEQUER-WORK	an alternating use of coloured brick squares, often black and red, or stone and flint, resembling a chess-board, often found in East Anglia.
CHEVET	French term for the east end of a church including chancel, ambulatory and radiating chapels. The best English example is at Westminster Abbey (see Figure 18).
CHEVRON	zig-zag ornament found in Norman work.
CHINOISERIE	decoration to evoke a feeling of China. It affected furniture and porcelain as well as architecture where pagodas, tea houses and pavilions became popular.
CLERESTORY	upper storey of nave, choir, and transept walls pierced by windows.
COFFERING	ceiling decoration of recessed square or polygonal ornamental panels.
COVING	the curving of the side of ceilings above the wall cornice to give an added dimension, as in the Double Cube Room at Wilton House.
CORBEL	block of stone beneath roof eaves, or to support wall shafts. Often they were carved with figurative decoration.
CORNICE	a projecting ledge forming the top section of the entablature in Classical architecture.
CROCKET	leaf-like decoration sprouting from the sloping sides of spires, pinnacles, gables, etc.
CROSSING	space at intersection of nave, chancel and transepts; in a cathedral often marked by a central tower as at Canterbury and York.
CUSP	projecting point between the foils in Gothic tracery.
DIAPER WORK	surface wall decoration composed of square or lozenge shapes.
DOG-TOOTH	Early English ornament consisting of a series of four leaves converging to a point to form a star-shaped pattern, set between moulded bands.
DOME	a vault over a circular or polygonal base, semicircular, segmented, pointed, or bulb-shaped in section. Often raised on a drum, e.g. St Paul's Cathedral (Figure 71).
DORMER	window placed vertically in the slope of a roof; sometimes hidden by a balustrade.
EAVES	underpart of a sloping roof overhanging a wall.
ENGAGED COLUMNS	columns attached to, or partly sunk into, a wall.
ENTABLATURE	the whole of the horizontal members above a column comprising architrave, frieze and cornice in classical architecture.

ENTASIS	slight convex deviation from the vertical used on classical columns to prevent an optical illusion of concavity.
FAÇADE	the exterior face of a building.
FANLIGHT	window often semicircular and over a door. Often decorated with radiating glazing bars suggesting the shape of an opening fan.
FLÈCHE	slender spire of wood or lead on ridge of roof.
FLUSHWORK	decorative mixture of flint and dressed stone sometimes forming tracery patterns as in a number of East Anglian churches.
FLUTING	vertical channelling in the shafts of a column.
FOLIATED	leaf-shaped, of carving usually round capitals.
FRIEZE	middle division of a classical entablature.
GABLE	the end wall of a building, the top of which conforms to the shape of the roof behind or acts as a brick screen. The edges are often dressed with stone coping (see drawings).
GALILEE	a porch or chapel at the west end of a church, e.g. Durham Cathedral.
GALLERY	a passage linking two major wings of a house; it could also be used for the display of family portraiture. Jacobean examples have intricate strapwork ornamented ceilings.
GARDEROBE	lavatory or privy in a medieval building.
GARGOYLE	projecting water spout often carved in the form of a human or animal face.
GAZEBO	summerhouse or belvedere in a picturesque garden. Common in the seventeenth and eighteenth centuries.
GIANT ORDER	classical ordered pilasters rising through two or more storeys. Used by Talman, Hawksmoor and Gibbs etc.
HALL	the principal living room of a medieval house. Also the main assembly room of a school, college, or court of justice.
HERRINGBONE WORK	brick, stone, or tile laid diagonally instead of in horizontal courses. Where alternate courses lie in opposing directions they create a zigzag pattern.
HEXASTYLE	a portico or centrepiece having six detached columns.
JAMB	straight side of an archway, window and doorway.
JETTY	the upper storeys of a house resting on projecting floor joists and so creating the effect of an overhang. The Shambles in York, and Mercery Lane, Canterbury, retain jettied buildings projecting over half the thoroughfare below.

KEEP	massive tower of a Norman castle; square, polygonal or circular, e.g. White Tower, Tower of London.
KEYSTONE	middle stone in an arch or a rib vault.
LADY CHAPEL	chapel dedicated to Our Blessed Lady usually to the east of the chancel. At Ely Cathedral it is to the north and almost detached.
LANCET ARCH	arch with acutely pointed head common in the Early Gothic period from about 1175.
LANTERN	a square or polygonal tower or structure in which all faces are pierced by large windows. When over a crossing the tower is open from below, as at York Minster.
LINTEL	horizontal beam or stone laid on two vertical posts thus bridging an opening. Stonehenge shows its most simple form.
LONG AND SHORT WORK	Saxon manner of wall cornering with stones placed with the long sides alternately upright and horizontal.
LOUVRE	opening, often with lantern over roof ridge to let smoke from central hearth escape.
LUCARNE	small opening in spire or a roof; in the former to allow air to circulate round timbers.
MACHICOLATIONS	a projecting gallery on castle walls or towers in which the floor is pierced by holes to allow the dropping of missiles onto an assailant below.
MASONRY	the craft of cutting, jointing and laying stone for building.
MASONRY SURFACES	see Figures 148-9.
MAUSOLEUM	monumental place of burial for family, so called after tomb of King Mausolus at Halicarnassus.
METOPE	in classical architecture of the Doric order, the panel in the frieze between the triglyphs.
MISERICORD	in choir stalls, a bracket on the underside of a hinged seat which allowed the occupant some support during long periods of standing.
MOTTE	a steep mound on which the stone keep of a castle was erected in the eleventh and twelfth centuries, e.g. York Castle.
NARTHEX	enclosed vestibule or covered porch against west front of church.
NEWEL	central post in a spiral staircase.
OBELISK	lofty pillar of square section tapering towards the top and ending in a point.

148 Treatment of stone wall surfaces.

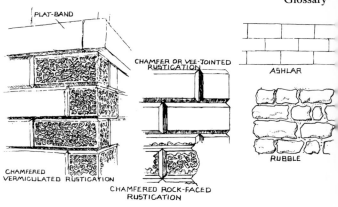

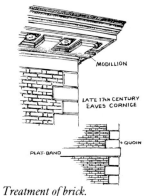

149 Treatment of brick.

OGEE

a semicircular arch which is pulled up into a point at its crown.

ORDER

in classical architecture it consists of column, with base, capital and entablature according to one of the following styles: Greek Doric, Roman Doric, Tuscan Doric, Ionic, Corinthian, Composite (see Figure 64).

ORIEL

window projecting from a façade at first storey or above.

PALLADIAN

architectural movement expounding the ideas and principles of Andrea Palladio 1508-80. Jones is considered the first disciple but the movement proper is eighteenth century, and spread to the Continent, as well as America.

PARAPET

low wall along edge of roof or piece of ground where there is a sudden drop. Often has the same purpose as a balustrade.

PEDIMENT

low-pitched gable used in Classical, Renaissance and Neo-classical architecture, above a portico, doors and windows. In the Baroque age they were often curved, and broken in the centre for a cartouche, or piece of sculpture.

PENDENTIVE	concave triangular spandrel used to direct the weight of a dome to one of four or eight piers. Wren's St Stephen, Walbrook, and St Paul's Cathedral have excellent examples.
PIANO NOBILE	principal storey of a house, usually emphasized by windows of greater height than on the other floors.
PIAZZA	open space surrounded by buildings. Italian in concept, it was brought to England by Inigo Jones and first used at Covent Garden in the 1630s.
PIER	arch or lintel support frequently square in section. In Romanesque, it often has attached shafts.
PILASTER	shallow rectangular column attached to a wall.
PINNACLE	ornamental form usually pyramidal and decorated with crockets at the summit of a buttress. On cathedrals they often act as a counterweight to the thrust of the flyer against the buttress.
PISCINA	basin for washing the Communion or Mass vessels provided with a drain. Set on the south wall of the chancel of a church and often adorned with moulding (see Figure 34).
PLAT-BAND	A horizontal band of ashlar stonework, slightly projecting from a façade.
PLINTH	projecting base of a wall or column.
PORTICO	centrepiece of a house or a church with Classical columns supporting an entablature and pediment.
PRESBYTERY	in cathedral or greater church planning, the part lying east of the choir in which the altar is placed.
PULPITUM	stone screen in a cathedral and abbey to shut off the choir from the nave, as in Canterbury Cathedral.
QUOINS	dressed stones at the angles of a building. They are usually placed in alternating courses of long or short blocks, and the edges may be chamfered, or cut away at an angle of 45° to the other two surfaces.
REREDOS	screen behind and above altar as in New College Chapel, Oxford.
ROOD	cross or crucifix.
ROOF	the construction of wood which affords a support for lead, tile or slates so covering the top of a building. In open-timbered roofs the framework can be admired, and adopts a number of constructional variations (see Figure 32).
RUSTICATION	courses of stone or brick with chamfered edges (see drawings of wall surfaces opposite).

ROSE WINDOW (or WHEEL WINDOW)	circular window with patterned tracery arranged to radiate from the centre. Excellent examples are at Lincoln Cathedral.
ROTUNDA	building circular in plan.
SANCTUARY	area around the main altar of a church; presbytery.
SEDILIA	seats for the priest and deacons (usually three) against the south wall of a chancel next to the piscina.
SOLAR	upper living room of a medieval house.
SPANDREL	the roughly triangular space formed by the curvature of an arch, the vertical wall shaft, and horizontal string course marking the arcade division.
SPIRE	pyramidal erection, generally octagonal in plan, placed on top of a tower.
SPLAY	chamfer or opening out of the jamb of a window, usually on the interior.
SQUINT	hole cut in wall or pier of chancel to allow view of main altar from adjacent chapel.
STEEPLE	the tower and spire of a church normally housing bells.
STIFF-LEAF	stylised foliage carving found on capitals and bosses during the Early English period.
STRAPWORK	sixteenth- and early seventeenth-century decoration, Flemish in origin, and consisting of interlaced bands like leather straps. Found on plaster ceilings as well as woodwork.
STRING COURSE	projecting horizontal band set into walls; it does not have the relief of a cornice.
STUCCO	plasterwork or fine-quality external rendering, often painted.
SWAG	festoon formed by a carved piece of cloth holding fruit or flowers and supported at each end.
TABERNACLE	richly ornamented niche or free-standing canopy. Also the receptacle for the sacrament in the centre of an altar, or to one side of the sanctuary.
TERM	classical sculptured figure whose lower half turns into a pedestal.
TERRACE	a row of houses joined together as a unified design, with the centre sometimes emphasized by a pediment. Also a raised space or platform in front of a building.
TIMBER-FRAMING	construction where basic structure is built of a timber framework with the space in between filled with brickwork or plaster; frequently the timber work has been covered with plaster, brick or tiles.

TRACERY	the intersecting stone framework of a Gothic window. The vertical strips are known as mullions, horizontal intersecting bars, transoms. Towards the head (top) of a window the tracery breaks into a decorative mesh of geometrical or flamboyant patterns.
TRANSEPT	transverse arm of a cruciform church.
TRIBUNE	gallery above aisles with arches opening to the nave.
TRIFORIUM	gallery with arches opening to nave and choir immediately below the clerestory.
TRIGLYPHS	blocks with vertical grooves separating the metopes in a Doric frieze.
TURRET	small tower (square, round, or polygonal) often found in military architecture.
TYMPANUM	space between the lintel of a doorway and the arch above it and in Norman period often adorned with carvings of Christ, as well as secular themes, e.g. Barfreston, Kent.
UNDERCROFT	a crypt or vault under a church or chapel.
VAULT – rib	an arched roof usually of stone in which the blocks filling the panels or cells are held in place by a web or ribs.
–tunnel or barrel	a continuous stone roof either semicircular or pointed in section.
–groin	two tunnel vaults of identical shape intersecting at right angles over a square bay as in Canterbury Cathedral western crypt.
VENETIAN ARCH	window with three openings of which the central one is larger and arched.
VERANDAH	open gallery with roof or canopy supported on light pillars often of cast iron.
VILLA	country house, usually a secondary and smaller residence of a wealthy family.
VOLUTE	curved corner scroll of an Ionic capital. Also a block of stone with serpentine curve forming one side and used as a decorative motif in Baroque architecture, e.g. St Martin's Ludgate, by Wren.
VOUSSOIR	wedge-shaped stone used in arch construction.
WAINSCOT	timber lining to walls.
WHEEL WINDOW	circular window with spoked tracery found in the Norman period. Sometimes also called a rose window, although this is really a later development in which the tracery assumes petal shapes.
ZIGZAG	Norman decoration known as chevron.

Bibliography

General
Allsop, B., *A General History of Architecture*, Pitman, 1960.
Barley, M.W. *The English Farmhouse and Cottage*, Routledge & Kegan Paul, 1961.
Clifton-Taylor, A., *The Pattern of English Building*, Faber, 1972.
Fleming, J., Honour, H. and Pevsner, N. *The Penguin Dictionary of Architecture*, Penguin, 1966.
Gardner, A.H., *Outline of English Architecture*, Batsford, 1946.
Girouard, M., *Life in the English Country House*, Yale University Press, 1978.
Kidson, P., Murray, P., and Thompson, P. *A History of English Architecture*, Penguin, 1962.
Lloyd, N., *History of the English House*, Architectural Press, 1931; rep. 1972.
Mercer, E., *English Vernacular Houses*, HMSO, 1975.
Statham, H.M., *A History of Architecture*, Batsford, 1950.
Tipping, H.A., *English Houses* (9 vols 1066-1820), Country Life, 1921.
Watkin, D., *English Architecture – A Concise History*, Thames & Hudson, 1979.
West, T.R., *English Architecture*, University of London, 1970.
Yarwood, Doreen, *The Architecture of England*, Batsford, 1963.

Medieval
Allen Brown, R., *The Architecture of Castles: A Visual Guide*, Batsford, 1984.
Braun, H., *An Introduction to English Medieval Architecture*, Faber, 1951.
Harvey, J. *Gothic England*, Batsford, 1948.
Harvey, J. *English Medieval Architects: a Biographical Dictionary*, Batsford, 1954.
Harvey, J. *The Perpendicular Style*, Batsford, 1978.
Godfrey, W.H., *Some Famous Buildings and their Story*, Technical Journals Ltd, 1911.
Platt, C., *The English Medieval Town*, Secker & Warburg, 1976.
Salzman, L.F., *Building in England Down to 1540*, Oxford, 1952.
Smith, J.T., Faulkner P.A., and Emery, A., *Studies in Medieval Architecture*, Royal Archaeological Institute, 1975.
Taylor, H.M. and J., *Anglo-Saxon Architecture*, Cambridge, 1965.
Toy, S., *The Castles of Great Britain*, Heinemann, 1963.
Webb, G., *Architecture in Britain: The Middle Ages*, Penguin, 1956.
Wood, Margaret, *The English Medieval House*, Phoenix House, 1965.

Sixteenth to eighteenth century
Colvin, H.M., *A Biographical Dictionary of British Architects 1600-1840*, John Murray, 1978.
Downes, K., *English Baroque Architecture*, Zwemmer, 1966.
Downes, K., *Hawksmoor*, Thames & Hudson, 1969.
Downes, K., *The Georgian Cities of Britain*, Phaidon, 1979.
Dutton, R., *The Age of Wren*, Batsford, 1951.
Fleming, J., *Robert Adam and his Circle*, John Murray, 1962.
Hill, O. and Cornforth, J., *English Country Houses, Caroline 1625-85*, Country Life, 1966.

Hussey, C., *English Country Houses: 1 Early Georgian, 1715-1760*, Country Life, 1955-8.
              2 Mid Georgian, 1760-1800, Country Life, 1955-8.
              3 Late Georgian, 1800-1840, Country Life, 1955-8.
Lees Milne, J., *The Age of Adam*, Batsford, 1947.
Lees Milne, J., *Tudor Renaissance*, Batsford, 1951.
Lees Milne, J., *The Age of Inigo Jones*, Batsford, 1953.
Lees Milne, J., *English Country Houses: Baroque 1685-1715*, Country Life, 1970.
Mercer, E., *English Art, 1553-1625*, Oxford, 1962.
Saxl, F. and Wittkower, R. *British Art and the Mediterranean*, Oxford, 1948.
Sitwell, S., *British Architects and Craftsmen 1600-1830*, Batsford, 1948.
Summerson, J., *Architecture in Britain 1530-1830*, Penguin, 1953.
Summerson, J., *Inigo Jones*, Penguin, 1966.
Whiffin, M., *Stuart and Georgian Churches 1603-1837*, Batsford, 1948.
Whinney, M. and Millar, O. *English Art 1625-1714*, Oxford, 1957.
Whinney, M., *Sir Christopher Wren*, Thames & Hudson, 1971.

Nineteenth- and twentieth-century architecture

Campbell, K., *Home Sweet Home, London County Council Domestic Architecture*, Academy/G.L.C., 1976.
Clark, B., *Church Building of the Nineteenth Century*, S.P.C.K., 1938.
Clark, K., *The Gothic Revival*, John Murray, 3rd edn, 1962.
Dixon, R. and Muthesius, S., *Victorian Architecture*, Thames & Hudson, 1978.
Furneaux Jordan, R., *Victorian Architecture*, Penguin, 1966.
Girouard, M., *The Victorian Country House*, Oxford, 1971.
Goodhart-Rendel, H.S., *English Architecture since the Regency*, Constable, 1953.
Hitchcock, Henry-Russell, *Architecture: Nineteenth and Twentieth Centuries*, Penguin, 1971.
Maxwell, R., *New British Architecture*, Thames & Hudson, 1972.
Mordaunt Crook, J., *The Greek Revival*, John Murray, 1972.
Pevsner, N., *Pioneers of Modern Design*, Penguin, 1960.
Richards, J.M., *An Introduction to Modern Architecture*, Penguin, 1940.
Richards, J.M., *The Functional Tradition in Early Industrial Buildings*, Architectural Press, 1975.
Service, A. (ed.), *Edwardian Architecture and its Origins*, Architectural Press, 1975.
Service, A. *Edwardian Architecture*, Thames & Hudson, 1977.
Summerson, J. *Victorian Architecture*, Columbia University Press, 1970.

Abbeys and cathedrals

Batsford, H. and Fry, C., *The Cathedrals of England*, Batsford, 1960.
Bond, F., *Gothic Architecture in England*, Oxford, 1906.
Bond, F., *The Cathedrals of England and Wales*, Oxford, 1912.
Bond, F., *An Introduction to English Church Architecture*, Oxford, 1913.
Cook, G.H., *The English Cathedrals through the Centuries*, Phoenix House, 1957.
Cook, G.H., *English Monasteries in the Middle Ages*, Phoenix House, 1961.
Cook, O. and Smith, E., *English Abbeys and Priories*, Thames & Hudson, 1960.
Crossley, F.H., *The English Abbey*, Batsford, 1949.
Harvey, J., *English Cathedrals*, Batsford, 1950.
Hurliman, M., *English Cathedrals*, Thames & Hudson, 1961.
Nicholson, C.B., *England's Greater Churches*, Batsford, 1949.
Swaan, W., *The Gothic Cathedral*, Elek, 1969.

Vale, E., *Abbeys and Priories*, Batsford, 1955.
Willis, R., *Architectural History of Some English Cathedrals (1842-63)*, Minet Reprints, 1972.

Parish churches
Clark, B., *The Building of the Eighteenth-century Church*, S.P.C.K., 1963.
Clifton-Taylor, A., *English Parish Churches as Works of Art*, Batsford, 1974.
Cobb, G., *The Old Churches of London*, Batsford, 1942.
Cook, G.H., *Medieval Chantries and Chantry Chapels*, Dent, Phoenix House, 1947.
Cook, G.H., *The English Medieval Parish Church*, Phoenix House, 1954.
Cook, G.H., *English Collegiate Churches*, Dent, Phoenix House, 1959.
Crossley, F.H., *English Church Design*, Batsford, 1945.
Foster, R., *Discovering English Churches*, Oxford University Press, 1982.
Rodwell, W., *The Archaeology of the English Church*, Batsford, 1982.
Smith, E., and Hutton, G., *English Parish Churches*, Thames & Hudson, 1952.
Smith, E., and Cook, O., *British Churches*, Dutton Vista, 1964.
Whiffin, M., *Stuart and Georgian Churches 1603-1837*, Batsford, 1947.
Vale, E., *Churches*, Batsford, 1954.

Specific buildings and architectural topography
The most detailed studies of individual buildings are to be found in appropriate volumes of the Victoria County Histories, and the Royal Commission on Historical Monuments inventories; the latter are also most useful for photographs of architectural detail.

R.C.H.M. volumes outstanding for the breadth of material are:
City of Cambridge   2 vols
City of Edinburgh   1 vol.
London   5 vols
City of Oxford   1 vol.
Salisbury   1 vol.
Stamford   1 vol.
City of York   5 vols.

The volumes of the Buildings of England series are admirable as pocket handbooks for the student, although sometimes even major buildings receive only brief mention. Most volumes have been revised since publication. Pitkin Pride of Britain books are of excellent value and the photographs can often compare with any in the most expensive publications.

Individual studies of specific towns and cities are almost too numerous to mention although the following are recent major studies in this field.
Hobhouse, H., *Lost London*, Macmillan, 1971.
Ison, W., *The Georgian Buildings of Bath*, 1948, reprinted by Kingsmead Reprints, 1969.
Ison, W., *The Georgian Buildings of Bristol*, Faber, 1952.
Linstrum, D., *The Historic Architecture of Leeds*, Oriel Press, Newcastle, 1969.
Liverpool City Planning Department, *Buildings of Liverpool*, 1978.
R.C.H.M., *Beverley: An Archaeological and Architectural Study*, H.M.S.O., 1982.
Summerson, J., *Georgian London*, 3rd ed, Barrie & Jenkins, 1978.
Youngson, A.J., *The Making of Classical Edinburgh*, Edinburgh University Press, 1966.

Index

Places

References to drawings are printed in italics; those to photographs are printed in bold type.

General